RELIGION AND
AMERICAN PUBLIC LIFE

RELIGION AND AMERICAN PUBLIC LIFE

Interpretations and Explorations

---

edited by

ROBIN W. LOVIN

PAULIST PRESS
New York/Mahwah

Acknowledgements
The Publisher gratefully acknowledges the use of the following articles
reprinted with permission:

"Religion and Reason in American Politics," by Franklin Gamwell, which
first appeared in THE JOURNAL OF LAW AND RELIGION, Vol. II,
No. 2, and "A Sort of Republican Banquet," by Martin E. Marty, which
first appeared in the JOURNAL OF RELIGION, Vol. 59, No. 4, October
1979, pp. 383–405. © 1979 by The University of Chicago.

Library of Congress Cataloging-in-Publication Data
Religion and American public life.

   Includes bibliographies.
   Contents: Religion and American public life /
Robin W. Lovin—The meaning of public life / Richard J.
Bernstein—Religious sensibility and the reconstruction
of public life / Douglas Sturm—[etc.]
   1. United States—Religion—1960–   . 2. United
States—Civilization—1970–   . I. Lovin, Robin W.
BL2525.R45   1986   291.1'71'0973   86-12318
ISBN 0-8091-2815-2 (pbk.)

Published by Paulist Press
997 Macarthur Boulevard
Mahwah, New Jersey 07430

Printed and bound in the
United States of America

Contents

v

CONTENTS

PART TWO
EXPLORATIONS

Foreword

Martin E. Marty

RELIGION IN THE WESTERN WORLD delicately balances its private and public faces. The impetus of biblical thought is to keep the two in tension. People will not respond to the sacred or be faithful to what they experience as the divine if they do not find their inmost needs addressed. They must make sense of an apparently random universe. They have to endow their sorrows and their joys with meaning. Religion has to speak to them in the long night watches, in times of private terror and personal joy, or it will not speak to them at all.

The religion that has predominated in the West, however, whether following the impulses of prophetic Judaism or the motifs of Christian apostolates, has always seen that purely private faith is incomplete. Worse than that, because it serves only the purposes of those who hold it and comes under no scrutiny or judgment, it can easily become idolatrous. The test of faith is under the light of public interchange, and the achievement of religion must include a reasonably successful encounter in the marketplace, the forum of ideas, the arena where human suffering is most visible, where the demand for service is greatest.

1

Americans, like other people, have had difficulty living with the tension between public and private in religion. During the 1970s, for example, in some reaction to what they felt was overexposure to the public order, many citizens undertook spiritual journeys that provided them with measures of meaning. Yet by the end of the decade, a large and thoughtful minority began to ask whether the direction they were taking was faithful to the message they claimed to be following. They began to ask again questions of public order, public discourse, and public service.

In response to these questions, some factions interpreted "public" to mean merely and purely "political," and undertook aggressive moves in order to have their view of God's will and morality to be regulative in all society. This straight-out political interpretation of what it meant to be public led them to see religious forces chiefly as power blocs, to separate "the children of light" from "the children of darkness" and to use their sectarian norms to measure who had or did not have legitimate places in civil society. Their approach was but one of many options for religious people to take as they faced the public.

More expansive alternatives are also available. It is possible to be faithful to one's private or communal vision in a subculture and still to see purpose and value in the larger culture, where most people do not share the roots or the implications of such a vision. This more tense and delicate approach has lacked articulators in recent years, at a time when the need to combine commitment and civility, in America and elsewhere, has become especially urgent.

No one individual or institution can provide the model for all that religion should mean and do in the public order. But responsible people make use of their personal gifts and institutional mandates. As a research arm of a university divinity school, the Institute for the Advanced Study of Religion at the University of Chicago Divinity School has determined to concentrate on some of the intellectual dimensions of the theme. In response to mindless activity, troubled and discriminating minds must serve as monitors. To sustain mindful programs, there must be people who bring together those who have ideas which might even improve them. To this end, the Institute is devoting much of its energy over a three year period to a Project on Religion and American Public Life.

Assisted by a grant from the Henry R. Luce Foundation, Institute leaders have already sponsored a major conference on "Religion and the Future of American Public Life," and convened an interdisciplinary faculty seminar that regularly brings researchers together to share work in progress. From time to time, the Project will issue book-length reports whose design it is to stimulate reaction, civil argument, and further research—always with the end that these ideas may have an impact on public activity.

This book combines some of the first results of the Project's inquiries. The three papers by Lovin, Bernstein, and Sturm were prepared for the conference on "Religion and the Future of American Public Life," held in March 1982. Here the authors were able to press further their own lines of research for a largely academic audience. Together with Franklin Gamwell's paper, "Religion and Reason in American Politics,"[1] these essays present comprehensive views of the role religion has played in American life and suggest terms for its place in the American future. They have, I think, succeeded in doing this in terms that also have currency among several publics beyond the academy.

A second set of three brief papers explore more specific dimensions of religion in American public life. Lovin, Tracy, and Marty[2] focus on the problems of a discussion that includes religious themes, and on the images of a republican public or a covenanted community that could accommodate that discussion. Many of the ideas in these essays were shaped in a series of downtown Chicago seminars for professionals from law, commerce, public service, and the like. Supported by a grant from the Association of Theological Schools, these seminars have tested the ideas of theological scholars among this wider audience. Uneasy with simple solutions and eager to refine their own reflections, the participants in each seminar have come forward with their own ideas, some of them countering those of the speakers and all of them providing grist for subsequent seminars. This is a way of saying that readers who find stimulus in this book should be alerted to watch for more.

No one has the sole key to the ways that religion and the public should meet in a kinetic, pluralist society. The mix is too rich, the set of situations is too volatile, and the repository of plausible proposals from many sources is too well-stocked to permit anyone's sense of having arrived at full resolutions. John Courtney Murray defined the public as "people locked in civil argument." From this argument they move to some creative disagreements. Out of these come the occasional agreements that give thoughtful people hope in the midst of confusion. In that spirit of hope we submit these essays to a reading public.

Notes

1. Franklin Gamwell's essay previously appeared in the *Journal of Law and Religion*, 2 (1984), 325–42.

2. Martin Marty's essay previously appeared in the *Journal of Religion*, 59 (October, 1979), 383–405.

PART ONE

INTERPRETATIONS

Religion and American Public Life: Three Relationships

ROBIN W. LOVIN

AN UNUSUALLY LARGE NUMBER of controversies in public life today have an explicitly religious dimension. Protesters who block access to military installations and congregations who shelter refugees from Central America cite biblical principles to justify their defiance of civil law. Catholic bishops knit their questions about nuclear deterrence, opposition to abortion, and rejection of capital punishment into a "seamless garment" of theological interpretation of the foundations of human rights. Conservative Protestants seek prayer in public schools and religious symbols in public places, while they mount specific challenges to the "secular humanism" of the public school curriculum.

In many of these controversies, of course, there are participants whose principal concerns are not religious, but political, moral, or economic. Nonetheless, the importance of religious groups as centers for organization and recruitment of activists, and the emphasis on explicit religious warrants for action suggest the need for a new examination of relationships between religious traditions, civil authorities, and individual judgments of conscience. What happens to a Christmas display in a suburban village square or the outcome of a protester's trial for trespassing on federal property may be of small significance compared to, say, the outcome of arms control negotiations, or even the fluctuations in the prime interest rate. If, however, these separate incidents point to larger changes in how Americans understand public life and the role of religion in it, then the significance of these items on the third and fourth pages of the daily newspaper may actually be greater than that of the events that grab the headlines on page one.

It is this import for the future of public life generally that is neglected in most treatments of these issues. Immediate concerns gravitate toward the policy choices involved: How shall abortion be regulated? Who may have access to the public schools? How far may a citizen's conscientious objections to defense policy go? What we overlook is that in our national history, the public forum where these questions are asked and answered has been shaped in part by the religious convictions that persons bring to public questions. Religion not only suggests answers to public moral questions. It also determines how people will participate in the discussion. Conflicts over seemingly unimportant local issues may have great significance if they portend demands for larger freedom to live by the standards of one's own faith or for public conformity to the standards of a religious morality.

My project in this essay is to focus attention on this relationship between religion and public life which lies behind the particular controversies that demand more immediate attention. As there is controversy over the public choices themselves, so there is no unanimity on this question of the more basic relationship between religion and American public life, but there are some persistent patterns to the answers that have been given.

When American religious communities and religious leaders have tried to explain why it is important to relate faith to public life, they have given answers that can be summarized under three basic claims. For some, religion maintains order. The religious commitments we share provide a system of shared meanings which makes public moral choices possible, and without which even basic forms of civility and social restraint are jeopardized. For others, religion guarantees freedom. An awareness of a center of ultimate value beyond the claims of the state is a defense against totalitarianism. The idea that persons have rights given by God protects both individuals and their communities of identity against excessive claims by the government. For others still, religion provides the possibility for new forms of social justice. If past wrongs can be righted and social relationships reformed along new and more equitable patterns, that possibility depends in large part on the way that religious patterns of self-transcendence render a way of life subject to challenge by the moral claims of others, and give those who make such claims some confidence that they can be understood and received.

Religion, then, relates not only to the specific policy questions that come into public dispute, but also to the underlying beliefs about order, freedom, or justice in which the policy discussions are set. Just which of these beliefs is primary, and which is primarily related to religion is itself a matter of some dispute. It is possible to trace the shifting emphasis between order, freedom, and justice in American religious history, but it is important to note, too, that order, freedom, and justice all have their advocates in American religion today. I propose to make a case for the contemporary importance of religion's role in social justice, but that case can be seen clearly only if we see it in the context of the alternatives.

ORDER

One historic understanding of the relationship between religion and American public life points to an essential role for religion in maintaining the patterns of authority and obedience which allow organized human life to continue. The conviction that a society without religion is a society on the verge of chaos had its high point in the West before the American experience began, and it has always been subject to question on these shores. As a people, we have been somewhat fearful of an alliance between the forces of religion and public order, largely because our liberal, contractarian political philosophy suggests that rational self-interest alone is sufficient to provide the minimum requirements of order.

In recent American religious thought, however, Reinhold Niebuhr forcefully challenged these liberal preconceptions.[1] He insisted that the social order on which we all depend is a fragile human creation, not to be taken for granted, and he reminded us that while barbarians are dependably self-interested, we cannot count on them always to be rational. So Niebuhr insisted that if government is to maintain order, it must have a quality of majesty. It must inspire a primitive awe that paves the way for cooperation and obedience, but it must also convey the impression that this power is in service of some worthy ideal, such as justice or the common good, and not simply an extension of the whim of the ruler.

Niebuhr's political realism penetrates the myths employed by sovereign powers with critical insight, to demonstrate that the universal values they espouse are closer to self-interest than they like to pretend, but the same critique that shows that every myth is partly false also shows that all of them express a truth about the religious basis of social order. Once order is no longer seen as the dependable outcome of rational self-interest, a public role for religion is at once assured. Not only is it the original locus of that sense of awe which majesty must evoke; religion is also the most comprehensive framework of shared meanings in the culture. It is this which provides the essential element for lifting majesty above mere force, and without it no one would have the motivation to suspend individual desires in favor of abstractions like justice or the common good. Appeals to rational self-interest work, if they work at all, because a religious system has already given what Clifford Geertz calls an "aura of factuality"[2] to the sustaining moral concepts for which a philosophy of enlightened self-interest can then provide a reductive explanation.

The Niebuhrian realist's insistence that the foundations of social order lie deeper than prudential calculations of self-interest and mutual advantage challenges the assumptions of American political liberalism and directs our attention to earlier and sometimes neglected connections between religion and order. The same theme appears in the anti-utopian bias of political realists who appreciate the fragility of the social order we have achieved and would rather not risk it in some gamble for revolutionary change. It is found in the aggressive effort to define and maintain community standards by the Moral Majority and other groups on the "new religious right," but it is also present in Richard Neuhaus' critical assessment of the secularism that has removed the symbols of shared values from our public life and created the vacuum that the right-wing movements are rushing in to fill.[3]

Concern for relationship between religion and social order need not imply a conservative commitment to the social status quo. Robert Bellah's understanding of "civil religion," indeed, implies quite the opposite. He sees in America today a society which depends so heavily on economic rationality and global hegemony that it is systematically undercutting the framework of shared meanings which are required for its survival. Only some radical social change—if such a change is still possible—

will permit the reappearance of a meaningful language of commitment that public life requires.[4] Bellah's prescriptions tend to be radical: industrial democracy, alternative communities for work and living, and a more restrained American outreach in the world arena; but his identification of the problem echoes that of more conservative voices who lament the loss of widely-shared religious symbols. Americans are increasingly centered on their own satisfactions. They have no meaningful idea of self-transcendence, and consequently they are less and less able to practice the forms of discipline and self-restraint that society requires for its survival.

It is in Bellah's work, indeed, that we see most clearly the key element in the connection between religion and social order. There is no single religious idea or specific set of symbols that, in itself, provides that connection. If those who are concerned about this relationship between religion and American public life speak primarily in Christian and, indeed, Puritan, Protestant symbols, that is largely due to historical accident. What is important is that there be some set of meanings that are shared, that provide a language of commitment which can be widely understood to values which are larger than personal purposes. For all the important differences between them, the Moral Majority and the sociologists of civil religion have in common the conviction that a culture survives and functions only on the basis of a specific set of meanings that everyone can share. Religion, which has a widely acknowledged capacity to invest those meanings with reality and intersubjective power, has the public role of contributing to social order by supporting the framework of shared meanings.

FREEDOM

The important link between religion and order has been expounded by a number of distinguished commentators. It remains, however, a minority report among the ways of relating religion and society in America. If the European religious establishments that emerged after the Reformation preserved social unity by excluding or regulating dissent, most American churches would identify their history with the excluded. The mainstream of American religious sentiment left Massachusetts Bay with Roger Williams in 1636 and has ever since regarded *freedom* as the most important contribution of religion to public life. The American churches, as Bonhoeffer perceptively noted, are churches of refugees, churches of exiles, not martyrs. They are communities of people who "took upon themselves the struggle of colonization so as to be able to live out their faith in freedom without a struggle."[5] That is clearly true of the waves of European Protestants who founded the major American denominations. It is true also for many black churches, who chose a path of institutional separation as a response to their subordination in the white churches. The role of the exile seeking a place to live a faith in freedom fits much of American Judaism. What is surprising is that the pattern also fits American Catholicism so well. Although the European Catholic hierarchy expended its energies until well into the nineteenth century trying to recover its role as the religious agent of social order, the bishops of the American immigrant parishes discovered quickly that one claims a place in this culture not by providing a universal framework for social life, but by asserting the freedom to live one's particular faith. Claims to any kind of privileged role in society only aroused Nativist suspicions, and church leaders prudently concluded that freedom was all they could demand. The Americanization of Catholicism, indeed, began when leading bishops began to say that freedom was all they really needed.[6]

This remarkable consensus among religious communities that their faiths have not only survived, but flourished in an atmosphere of religious freedom leads, then, to the second principal relationship that has been maintained between religion and American public life, the idea that the public role of religion is to guarantee freedom. Religious groups in America not only defend their rights to their own beliefs; they defend the rights of other groups as well. By their very existence, these groups taken together secure a whole range of freedoms for all persons in the society.

It is not so easy to point to distinguished individual representatives of this point of view in our history, largely because the position has seldom needed public defense. It has been institutional orthodoxy in most American denominations from the beginning, though we must credit John A. Ryan and John Courtney Murray with making it respectable in the wider world of Roman Catholicism. Major systematic defenses of this position have, however, appeared rather recently, as events have called all of our cultural assumptions into question. The chief defenses of religious freedom, in fact, have been mounted by post-Vatican II Catholics who have turned a critical eye on the universalizing claims of earlier moral theology and have a new consciousness of themselves as members of a particular religious community. Alongside these, we find powerful contemporary defenses of religious freedom on the part of sectarian Protestants, who find the understanding of the social role of religious minority that they have inherited from their sixteenth century Anabaptist forebears curiously well-suited to the conditions of life in a pluralistic, secular society.[7]

This affinity in social thought between Catholics and sectarian Protestants, like the similarities we noted earlier between "civil religion" and Protestant conservatism, remind us

again that the understandings of religion and public life which
we are tracing in this essay are not tied to particular theologies,
symbol systems, or denominational histories. Rather, it seems
that a wide variety of religious groups, confronting under different conditions and at different points in time the individualism and economic rationalism of the dominant liberal
tradition in America, have found appropriate responses within
a rather limited repertoire of social ideas. These ideas, then,
link them to other groups who have adopted similar strategies,
despite apparent differences in history and theology.

What characterizes those who have emphasized the connection between religion and freedom is their emphasis on the
religious community, on its faith and way of life that unite its
members and distinguish them from the rest of the society.
There is here none of the appeal to shared cultural meanings
that marks "civil religion." The system of meanings which
makes morality possible belongs to the gathered community,
to those who explicitly identify themselves with the faith that
preserves the religious meanings, primarily in narrative form.

The emphasis on narrative and community gives a particularity to moral discourse which means that moral claims in
their most complete form simply cannot be made in public
terms. Attempts to talk about abortion, for example, fail because the public forums of legislature and law courts simply
cannot admit the affective, narrative arguments by which
Christians establish for themselves that nascent, helpless human life is precious in the sight of God. This does not mean
that Christians and other religious groups cannot accomplish
their purposes by effective use of the political process, but it
does mean, as Stanley Hauerwas warns, that they must not
make the mistake of supposing that political success means that
their underlying argument has been heard and accepted.[8]

One problem with this emphasis on freedom is that it
seems to depend implicitly on the idea that there are very few

problems that require choices that are at once public and moral. Although the proponents of freedom would surely deny it, there seems to be a residual liberalism in the idea that the limited number of really necessary public decisions can be made in such a way that nobody will be unduly inconvenienced by the results, and the communities of identity will be able to go about their distinct ways of life with a minimum of interference. Under ordinary political circumstances in Western democracies, where religious groups have opportunities to advocate their positions in public forums, it seems strange for a community to give up on that process from the outset, unless it is convinced that nothing really important is going to be decided in public anyway.

Those who see religion's public role as a guarantee of freedom would probably reply that the present political circumstances are not ordinary, even in apparently secure Western democracies, to say nothing of the more difficult circumstances that communities of faith face under totalitarian regimes around the world. In the political theology of Johann Baptist Metz, for example, stress on the role of the church as a self-conscious community of shared meanings correlates with a sense that the larger political scene is an arena of meaningless power.[9] The dominant systems, bourgeois and soviet, rest on power alone, strengthen themselves by exploitation of the poor, and sustain their hold on the people by systematic deceptions that convey an impression of their own virtue and provoke fear of the rival system. Under these circumstances, the present danger that all persons face is totalitarianism, whether of the left or the right. That is to say that what the advocates of freedom most fear is precisely what the partisans of order want: a single system of meanings to which everyone in the culture may and must subscribe, which gains its power to guide and motivate action by overshadowing more particular commitments with its own impression of ultimate reality and power.

In the face of that danger, religious communities become guarantors of public freedom by the mere fact of their existence. So long as they are there, no totalitarian power can plausibly claim that there are no centers of meaning and value outside of its own ideology. Paradoxically, religion serves its public purpose by turning its back on the public. There may be strategic sorties into politics or the media, but the communities of faith do their best to insure freedom for all by attending to themselves, by preserving the narratives that give them identity and forming persons of character whose lives and actions are appropriate to the stories they tell. This emphasis on the particularity of each community of faith largely relieves the problem of differences between them. Since no community seeks a monopoly on meaning, none needs to be disturbed by the presence of others, nor is there any pressure to find common symbols or minimal affirmations that might serve as the basis for a "civil religion." The public role of religion as the guarantee of freedom is actually enhanced by the existence of a plurality of systems of meaning. Religious unity is an eschatological or "messianic" hope. For the present, the communities do their public work best by accentuating their individual identities. So Metz calls, cautiously, for a ". . . *coalition of messianic trust* between Jews and Christians in opposition to the apotheosis of banality and hatred present in our world. Indeed, the remembrance of Auschwitz should sharpen all our senses for present-day processes of extermination in countries in which on the surface 'law and order' reigns as it did once in Nazi Germany."[10]

The remarkably firm historical commitment of American religious institutions to this public role of securing freedom probably does not rest on quite so baleful a view of public life as recent political theology suggests. Indeed, the commitment may rather be due to the convenient fact that this is the one public role a denomination can fill precisely by maintaining a visible institutional system and a vigorous institutional life. Nevertheless, it is certainly true that a remarkably broad spectrum of religious groups, from the Church of the Brethren to Roman Catholics, stand ready to oppose any explicit intrusion of religion into the established legal order quite as vigorously as they would oppose state intervention in the affairs of their churches.

JUSTICE

So we are faced with the odd fact that the social thinking of persecuted sectarians and religious exiles has become the dominant conception of religion's public role in the Western world's most religious nation. Indeed, it might have held that position undisputed, were it not for the emergence at several points in our history of groups who found that the freedom to form one's own identity and one's own community is not enough. Religious abolitionists before the Civil War, the social gospel movement at the beginning of this century, and most recently the civil rights movement as it grew out of the black churches all became dissidents from the common public role of religion as the guarantee of freedom, and as they did so, they were often perceived as threats to the religious foundations of public order. The actual point of their social agitation was somewhat different, and examination of it leads us to the third major role of religion in American public life, religion as a faith in the possibility of social justice.

What these groups have in common, despite the diversity of their aims and histories, is a commitment to ideas that could not be lived out freely in any of the existing frameworks of shared meaning. At some point, for the laborer trudging to begin a ten hour day in a noisy and unsafe factory, talk about the dignity of labor and the sacred responsibilities of family life is not enough. At some point, for a black woman ordered to the back of a crowded bus, the sustaining Sunday morning talk of one's freedom as a child of God will no longer suffice. What these persons share, together with the preachers and theologians who became their advocates, is a sense that they have a rightful claim against the rest of society. That claim is deeply rooted in their community of faith, and it becomes a part of the system of meaning that the community shares, but it is clear that by its very nature the claim cannot be satisfied merely by being nurtured in a community. It demands recognition by the rest of society as well.

A variety of strategies have been used to gain this recognition. The efforts of black Americans to obtain full citizenship rights have relied heavily on the courts, with a concerted campaign for educational equality that began in the 1930s and extended in later decades into litigation to eliminate de facto segregation of public housing and to secure compensatory programs for the victims of previous discrimination. Litigation, however, tends to culminate in legislation, as people seek more comprehensive programs to consolidate the gains of widely scattered court decisions; and litigation and legislation alike are often coupled with campaigns of public persuasion that seek to ground the demands for justice in American traditions or a general public sense of fair play.

We cannot here attempt to evaluate the practical effects of this characteristically American combination of rhetoric, politics, and litigation, or to assess the relative importance of each element of the strategy. What is important for present purposes is to see the difference between these strategic measures in a campaign for social justice and ordinary litigation or legislation. Ordinarily, an appeal to a jury, a judge, a city council, or a representative assembly implies that some framework of agreement, some set of shared meanings is already in place. If the shared meaning is no more than the common understanding that the complainants represent a body of votes or a bloc of economic interests that the legislator must take seriously come next election, still the assumption is that there is in place a set of linguistic, conceptual, and political institutions that can accommodate the claims of the protesters and provide the recognition they are seeking. Where the divisions are really serious, however, it is precisely that assumption that is in question. Whether in South Africa today, where the white minority government refuses to consider a conception of citizenship that would grant political equality to blacks, or at an earlier point in America when southern political leaders insisted that racial segregation was the very premise of the region's social life, or when courts and corporations joined in the nineteenth century in insisting that the unalterable institutions of private property and freedom of contract precluded the formation of labor unions, the critical challenges for the future of public life arise not when disagreements within a framework of shared meanings test the limits of government's capacity to keep order without destroying freedom, but when it becomes apparent that no framework of concepts or concrete social structures exists in which the justice that a group's self-understanding demands can be recognized by the wider society.

It is at just this point that the public role of religion as a commitment to the creative possibilities for justice becomes crucial. Religious traditions can provide individuals in communities that share narratives and values with the confidence that their demands are not merely their own wishes, but are grounded in the hope of the whole community and in its vision of justice. More important, however, is the fact that the religious traditions important in American life, the monotheistic faiths of Judaism and Christianity, have understood these hopes and visions to be grounded in a God who both supports and transcends the community of faith and its self-understanding. Demands for justice framed in the traditions of what H. Richard Niebuhr called "radical monotheism"[11] insist that they are not just the demands of a community and its tradition. They are grounded in a reality which demands recognition, even from those whose traditions and values may be quite different. However, because this reality not only supports, but also transcends the community and its demands, the justice that is sought can never be simply imposed by the community seeking recognition.

Those who understand their moral claims in these terms may be more insistent in their demands for recognition than those whose theories lead them to confine moral meanings to the communities who share a way of life in which the moral terms are used. In place of the modest claim that rationality is simply "the European intellectual's form of life,"[12] religious traditions typically assert some demands before which forms of life, whether of "European intellectuals" or others, must yield.[13] The demand, however, is not an assertion that the opposition will be *forced* to yield, but precisely the claim that despite the lack of any apparent framework in which the demands could now be recognized, the possibility of a new understanding is implicit in the claims themselves.

If Niebuhr's concept of "radical monotheism" correctly characterizes the way that major American religious traditions understand shared systems of meaning, it has important implications for the way that these communities can relate in a pluralistic society and for the possibilities of change in the midst of social conflict. Despite the current theological interest in narrative, language, and tradition, however, little attention has been given to the creation of shared meanings in the larger social context in which these communities must coexist.

Instead, the very success of American religious groups as

centers of meaning and freedom may contribute to the deterioration of public discussions about the claims we make on one another and about the choices we must make together. While the privatization of meaning in self-conscious communities of believer protects freedom for all of us by dispelling the illusion that some central authority could provide all of the common commitments we need, privatization may also lead us to consider important public choices meaningless. To insist that one cannot really explain one's actions in a public forum invites a positivistic view of the decisions that must, finally, be made in that forum. Once we are convinced that we cannot say what is truly important about the sanctity of life, about peace, or about justice in public, we have to confront the problem that nobody else can say it, either. Since we cannot simply stop taking action on abortion, defense policy, and civil rights, we find ourselves in the awkward position of making choices for which, in principle, no one has any really good reasons. The only solution is the unpalatable one first offered by Hobbes: we designate someone—or some institution, or some procedure—to make the decision for us, and we commit ourselves to follow that choice in order to avoid the nastiness that would ensue if we left the question unanswered.

The growth of single-issue politics and widespread attempts to choose judges and political leaders on the basis of their commitments on specific policy questions testify to a general loss of confidence in meaningful discussion in public life. The complicity, not to mention the sponsorship, of some religious groups in these movements suggests that our historic preoccupation with the connection between religion and freedom in public life may be leading us to overlook another relationship which is at least as important. The end result of our present direction is likely to be a social order balanced between the fragmented collection of communities who are able to speak meaningfully about ultimate questions (though only to those who already agree with them) and a state which makes proximate decisions that have no meaning at all, except perhaps as a scoresheet to tell who is currently most effective at manipulating the decision-making process.

The more clear-sighted partisans of freedom are not oblivious to this problem, but they see no way to avoid it without recourse to a society which imposes a common framework of meanings to secure social order. Given the reality of a pluralistic society, they see no way to give meaning to public discussion except by imposing it. Accordingly, they reject talk of religion's role in shaping new formulations of social justice as a sort of Constantinian nostalgia, a yearning for an order that can no longer be, and that we probably would not really want if we could have it.

A serious concern for religion and the possibility of social justice must begin, then, by confronting the problem of pluralism and the apparent fragmentation of moral meaning in American life. The challenge, of course, is not to make the pluralism go away, but to articulate more clearly the difficulties it creates for meaningful public discourse, in the hope that when the problems can be seen clearly, possibilities for solutions may also suggest themselves.

It is at this point that current theological interest in the public aspects of religious language[14] converges with systematic issues in social ethics, for this theological issue has at least this much in common with the problems of ethics in a pluralistic society: it must explain how a system of ideas apparently complete in itself and centered on a distinctive set of theological affirmations can be understood and even criticized by an observer who stands initially within another system, and who may never enter completely into the system under examination. There is no agreement among theologians how best to do this. Hermeneutics, Wittgensteinian "language games," Whiteheadian relationalism, and various forms of naive or sophisticated realism have all at one time or another provided methods for this inquiry. What all the efforts have in common, however, is that they account for the ways in which a meaning that originates in one particular community can be understood and incorporated into the ideas of another. In contrast to the tolerant but enervating suggestion of R.M. Hare that religious belief is a "blik" which makes sense only in its own terms and only as a whole,[15] the theologian seeks a way to make discrete truth claims which can be understood and evaluated without accepting everything that the theologian himself or herself believes. Such claims are not framed on the assumption that there is some vocabulary of universal rationalism. They retain their identity as part of the tradition of a particular community of faith. Neither are they framed as mystical insights incomprehensible or even self-contradictory to the uninitiated.

This view of religious language makes possible a quite different style of argument from the system which enforces as public truths the claims of a normative religious order. Christians, Jews, Muslims, and others may be aware of their distinctive identities, each acknowledging, as Barth put it, that on this side of the eschaton their faith is ". . . only one note among many other invocations and exclamations that are hardly in harmony with it, but call for notice just as loudly, or even more so."[16] Yet this does not preclude that elements of a faith can be recognized as true or its moral claims taken as guides for action in the experience of other communities as well. What is required is a criterion of public truth that is different from the criterion for a correct interpretation of one's own tradition, a criterion that requires corroboration of one's claims in the critical scrutiny of another community of meaning and which holds back from claims to this sort of truth until that corroboration is forthcoming.

Recent theological reflection on language provides an explanation of the conditions that make such public truth possible. The demonstration of this possibility is an important theoretical task at a time when much of the literature of religious ethics in America treats the options as a stark alternative between the "Constantinian" imposition of a religiously grounded social order and the sectarian religious defense of freedom.

A public role for religion which required the participants to understand the intricacies of hermeneutics or Whiteheadian metaphysics would, however, be a public role in serious trouble, so it is important to remind ourselves that these theoretical considerations merely confirm the plausibility of a way of public speaking and acting that some religious groups and individuals have followed all along. They have made claims, especially claims about justice, which did not suppose that everyone who heard them shared the religious experience in which the claims were formed. They have wagered their own lives and safety on the presumption that their claims could establish themselves as true in the experience even of those whose world of experience was quite different. They have been willing to wait for corroboration of their claims by the wider community, and though they have sometimes appealed for the corroboration from the immediate community in which they lived to a human community of wider extent in space and time, they have not resorted either to gaining their objectives by force or to stating their claims in a universalized form that denies their origins in the particularities of their own experience.

Religion which takes this public role strengthens the society which mediates between the particular communities of identity and the general coercive power of the state. Indeed, it requires this social matrix in which to make good its own claims for truth. In an American culture which seems to be more threatened internally by a positivism which drains public life of meaning than by a totalitarianism which loads it with an imposed and exclusive system of meanings, religion's most important public role may be to strengthen the society by a vigorous use of that forum, stressing the importance of questions that can be resolved neither by the power of the state nor in the confines of particular communities.

Perhaps our American past has allowed us to take this societal forum and its moral creativity too much for granted. Our mobility and our individualism have made it difficult to sustain even the more limited communities of identity, and our resources of space and material abundance have spared us many hard choices that other societies have had to make. We have not had to compete with one another, either for physical space or for space for our ideas, and out of that rather unrestrained exchange we have created solutions to our social and technical problems that no one could have envisioned in advance. Consequently, we have learned to fear above all else the too-quick answer and the heavy hand of totalitarianism that closes all social questions before they can be asked. Religion has played its part in this exuberant, creative social freedom, and religion has prospered in it, too. We have come to value open questions above dogmatic answers, and we are likely to continue to do so in the future; but the privatization of meaning and the drift of politics toward meaningless solutions imposed by the power of "majorities," moral or otherwise, should warn us that public questions stay open only when there is a social forum in which they can be raised with the expectation of a creative answer. Questions for which we are convinced that there is no answer are as closed as questions for which only one answer is allowed.

Notes

1. See, especially, Reinhold Niebuhr, *The Children of Light and the Children of Darkness* (New York: Scribner's, 1944), and *The Structure of Nations and Empires* (New York: Scribner's, 1959).

2. Clifford Geertz, *The Interpretation of Cultures* (New York: Basic Books, 1973), p. 90.

3. Richard John Neuhaus, *The Naked Public Square* (Grand Rapids: Eerdmanns, 1984), pp. 78–93.

4. See, most recently, Robert N. Bellah, Richard Madsen, William M. Sullivan, Ann Swidler, and Steven M. Tipton, *Habits of the Heart: Individualism and Commitment in American Life* (Berkeley: University of California Press, 1985), especially pp. 223–25. Bellah's own understanding of "civil religion" and the institutional problems of American society are also detailed in Robert N. Bellah, *The Broken Covenant: American Civil Religion in Time of Trial* (New York: Seabury Press, 1975), especially chapters 5–6.

5. Dietrich Bonhoeffer, *No Rusty Swords*, ed. Edwin H. Robertson (London: Collins, 1970), p. 98.

6. Sidney Ahlstrom, *A Religious History of the American People* (New Haven: Yale University Press, 1972), pp. 825–41.

7. For the Catholic position, see Enda McDonagh, *Doing the Truth* (Notre Dame, Indiana: University of Notre Dame Press, 1979). For the Protestants, see John Howard Yoder, *The Politics of Jesus* (Grand Rapids: Eerdmans, 1972).

8. Stanley Hauerwas, "Abortion: Why the Arguments Fail," in *A Community of Character* (Notre Dame, Indiana: University of Notre Dame Press, 1981), p. 229.

9. Johann Baptist Metz, *The Emergent Church* (New York: Crossroad, 1981).

10. *Ibid.*, p. 32.

11. H. Richard Niebuhr, *Radical Monotheism and Western Culture* (New York: Harper and Row, 1970), pp. 24–37.

12. Richard Rorty, *Consequences of Pragmatism* (Minneapolis: University of Minnesota Press, 1982), p. 172.

13. H.R. Niebuhr argues that the actual use of the language of

value follows this pattern in dealing with concrete ethical problems, despite what subjectivist or relativist theories of knowledge may affirm at a more general level. This seems to be a claim about the way moral language is used in fact, rather than a claim about how it must be used. One need not insist that *no one* uses moral language in any other way to accept Niebuhr's point that the understanding that moral claims both support and transcend the communities that make them is not confined to the monotheistic faith communities in which it is linked to central theological affirmations. See H.R. Niebuhr, *Radical Monotheism*, pp. 100–103.

14. See, especially, David Tracy, *The Analogical Imagination* (New York: Crossroad, 1981), and Tracy's essay in this volume.

15. See Hare's contribution to the discussion in Antony Flew and Alasdair MacIntyre, eds., *New Essays in Philosophical Theology* (New York: Macmillan, 1955), pp. 275–95.

16. Karl Barth, *The Christian Life* (Grand Rapids: Eerdmans, 1981), p. 7.

The Meaning of Public Life

RICHARD J. BERNSTEIN

WHAT ROLE, IF ANY, CAN RELIGION play in American public life? If we are to make any serious headway in answering this question, a number of prior issues need to be confronted. What are we really talking about? What do we (or what should we) mean by "public life," "American public life," and, of course, "religion"? My primary focus in this essay will be on the meaning of public life. This will enable me to turn to the issue of American public life and to raise some questions about religion and American public life. More specifically, I am concerned to clarify and help recover a concept of public life that has been distorted and obscured in recent times, and to argue that it is vitally relevant to our contemporary situation. I want to do this through a dialogical encounter with several thinkers who have spoken to this issue: Hans-Georg Gadamer, Jürgen Habermas, Hannah Arendt, and John Dewey. The meaning of public life has taken on global significance in our time. Although Gadamer and Habermas are not speaking directly to the American situation, their critiques of contemporary society are directed to a recovery of authentic public life. Hannah Arendt and John Dewey have spoken forcefully and eloquently about the crises and problems of American public life. I will be emphasizing some of the themes that these four thinkers share in common rather than the important and consequential differences that divide them.

One of the common themes shared by Gadamer, Habermas, and Arendt in their critiques of contemporary society has been the confusion and obliteration of the categorial distinction between the technical and the practical. Each has argued (with differing emphases) that the obliteration of this distinction has had devastating conceptual and practical consequences. The issue is not simply a conceptual or linguistic one—what underlies their critiques is the deformation of our very forms of life. Let me begin with some characteristic passages from each of these thinkers.

Gadamer, who has sought to recover and appropriate Aristotle's understanding of *praxis* and *phronesis* to *our* historical situation, and who has argued that hermeneutics is the heir to this tradition of practical philosophy, writes:

> In my own eyes, the great merit of Aristotle was that he anticipated the impasse of our scientific culture by his description of the structure of practical reason as distinct from theoretical knowledge and technical skill. By philosophical arguments he refuted the claim of the professional lawmakers whose function at that time corresponded to the role of the expert in the modern scientific society. Of course, I do not mean to equate the modern expert with the professional sophist. In his own field, he is a faithful and reliable investigator, and in general he is well aware of the particularity of his methodological assumptions and realizes that the results of his investigation have a limited relevance. Nevertheless the problem of our society is that the longing of the citizenry for orientation and normative patterns invest the expert with exaggerated authority. Modern society expects him to provide a substitute for past

moral and political orientations. Consequently, the concept of 'praxis' which has developed in the last two centuries is an awful deformation of what practice really is. In all the debates of the last century practice was understood as the application of science to technical tasks. . . . It degrades practical reason to technical control.[1]

Compare this with a characteristic claim of Habermas:

The real difficulty in the relation of theory and praxis does not arise from this new function of science as technological force, but rather from the fact that we are no longer able to distinguish between practical and technical power. Yet even a civilization that has been rendered scientific is not granted dispensation from practical questions: therefore a peculiar danger arises when the process of scientification transgresses the limit of technical questions, without, however, departing from the level of reflection of a rationality confined to the technical horizon. For then no attempt at all is made to attain a rational consensus on the part of the citizens concerned with the practical control of their destiny. Its place is taken by the attempt to attain technical control over history by perfecting the administration of society, an attempt that is just as impractical as it is unhistorical.[2]

Finally the threat posed by the domination of the technical, what Hannah Arendt called the victory of *homo faber*, is indicated when she writes:

Among the outstanding characteristics of the modern age from its beginning to our time we find the typical attitudes of *homo faber*: his instrumentalization of the world, his confidence in tools and in the productivity of the maker of artificial objects; his trust in the all-comprehensive range of means-end category, his conviction that every issue can be

solved and every human motivation reduced to the principle of utility; his sovereignty, which regards everything
as material and thinks of the whole nature as an 'immense
fabric from which we can cut out whatever we want to re-
sew it however we like,' his equation of intelligence with
ingenuity, that is, his contempt for all thought which cannot be considered to be 'the first step . . . for the fabrication of artificial objects, particularly of tools to make
tools, and to vary their fabrication indefinitely'; finally, his
matter-of-course identification of fabrication with action
[praxis].[3]

What each of these thinkers is locating is the all-encompassing tendency toward technical control, and, more fundamentally, the mentality that this exhibits. And each has sought
to show that there is a type of action and practical rationality
which is deformed when it is assimilated to the technical. They
have sought to get to the roots of the underlying epistemology,
the social forces, and the material conditions that support and
further this tendency. And each has seen how it has created a
moral and political vacuum where the type of public life in
which there can be genuine mutual dialogue and rational persuasion is undermined. This tendency can be viewed as the
dark side of the legacy of the Enlightenment. For while the
classic Enlightenment thinkers believed that with the triumph
of reason over superstition and prejudice human beings would
be able to achieve moral and political freedom, we have witnessed the perversion of this project in the modern world. We
have seen how "abstract reason" which sets out to *remake* society can and has led to grotesque forms of terror. Or, alternatively, we have seen how there has been a shrinkage of the
concept of reason which is limited to the effective or efficient
means for achieving pre-given ends, and where the only concept of "action" that seems to make sense is the technical ap-

plication of scientific knowledge. There has been a loss of confidence and a deep skepticism about the very possibility of a rational deliberation of the ends and norms that ought to govern our lives, and a deformation of the type of public space in which such practical discourse can take place.

This is a tendency that can be related to the Weberian thesis about the progressive "rationalization" of Western society and the consequent disenchantment of the world. For the triumph of the mentality of *zweckrationalität*—instrumental or goal-rationality—affects and infects every domain of human life.[4] Weber's vision of contemporary society was indeed bleak. For he thought not only that science was meaningless *in the sense* that it gives no answer to the question "What shall we do and how shall we live?" but also that there is no rational discipline that can fill the vacuum of lost moral and political orientations. The disenchantment of the world brought about by the progressive rationalization of society destroys traditional bases for moral and political orientations. There is no possibility of rationally justifying the ultimate norms that govern our lives. There is nothing that can lessen the burden and responsibility of choosing among the competing gods or demons that we follow. Weber was also prophetic about the failures of modern society—whether capitalist or socialist—in extricating us from the "iron cage" of the progressive bureaucratic rationalization of society. The consequences of this for politics and public life have been unmistakable, for what has taken place in our time is the "depolitization of the mass of the population and the decline of the public realm as a political institution."[5]

It is against this background that we can appreciate the deep concern of Gadamer, Habermas, and Arendt. Each has sought to recover a concept of public life, practical rationality, and *praxis* that might still speak to our contemporary situation. Each has resisted that form of totalizing thinking which despairs about the possibility of a recovery of public life. And in each there are similar themes that they stress in their analyses of the meaning of public life.

Gadamer, especially in his writings since *Truth and Method*, has returned over and over again to the fusion of hermeneutics and *praxis*, arguing that hermeneutics is properly understood when it is seen as the heir to the older tradition of practical philosophy, and has the primary task of defending practical and political reason against the domination of technology based on science. It seeks to vindicate once again "the noblest task of the citizen—decision-making according to one's own responsibility—instead of conceding the task to the expert."[6] His own understanding of practical reason or ethical know-how is a blending of motifs he has appropriated from classical philosophy: *phronesis* and *dialogue*. *Phronesis* cannot be reduced to technical know-how. It involves a distinctive mediation of the universal (norms and principles) to particular concrete situations. *Phronesis* is not the subsumption of particulars under pre-determined fixed rules. There is an essential openness and indeterminacy of all principles funded in the life of the community or *polis*. The virtue of *phronesis* requires judgment, deliberation, discernment, friendship and solidarity. Unlike "objective knowledge" which can be detached from the individual, practical knowledge shapes what we are in the process of becoming. It is a form of knowledge that becomes constitutive of our being. There is an "interlacing of being and knowledge, determination through one's own becoming, *Hexis*, recognition of the situational Good, and *Logos*."[7] Gadamer stresses that such practical knowledge can only be cultivated and transmitted through dialogue and conversation. "It is characteristic of every true conversation that each opens himself to the other person, truly accepts his point of view as worthy of consideration and gets inside the other to such an extent that he understands not a particular individual, but what he says.

The thing that has been grasped is the objective rightness or otherwise of opinion, so that they can agree with each other on the subject."[8] Gadamer's analysis of dialogue, questioning, and conversation has strong practical and political implications. For philosophical hermeneutics can itself be interpreted as showing that what is most essential about our humanity, what characterizes our being in the world, is to be dialogical. And while Gadamer stresses our dialogue, questioning, and conversation with tradition, it becomes clear for him that if such a dialogue is to become a living reality in our public life then it requires and fosters a mutual respect, and a serious willingness to test and risk one's own opinions. It requires a solidarity among participants—or, to use Hannah Arendt's phrase, a public space in which rational persuasion becomes a reality. "Practice," Gadamer tells us, "is conducting oneself and acting in solidarity."[9]

In this respect, despite the famous dispute between Gadamer and Habermas, Habermas does not so much disagree with Gadamer, but seeks to draw out the radical implications that are implicit in this conception of understanding as dialogical. Like Gadamer, Habermas has sought to show what is wrong with a concept of rationality and the rationalization of society which is limited to *zweckrationalität*. His universal pragmatics, his theory of communicative action, is intended to show that there is a distinctive type of communicative rationality that must be sharply distinguished from instrumental, strategic and technical reason. For communicative action is oriented to a mutual understanding among participants. "In contradistinction to purposive-rational action, communicative action, among other things, is oriented to observing intersubjective valid norms that link reciprocal expectations."[10] Rationalization on the level of communicative action and discourse means eliminating the relations of force and domination that distort communicative action. It means overcoming systematically distorted communication. For Habermas, this also points to a practical and political task. For he argues that communicative action itself presupposes and anticipates an ideal speech situation where there are no internal or external constraints except the force of the better argument. And this demands the material conditions in a society in which such undistorted communication is realized. For Habermas the idea of truth, especially practical truth, is intimately linked with the demand for a just society. A genuine public life for Habermas is not one that is characterized by manipulation, or the contest of individual or group or class interests, or overt or covert forms of domination, but is one where participants as equals can engage in practical discourse and decision-making.

What Gadamer seeks to clarify for us through his appropriation of *phronesis* and dialogue from classical philosophy, and what Habermas explores from the perspective of a comprehensive theory of communicative action, is approached in still another way by Hannah Arendt's vivid descriptions of the meaning of action, politics, and the type of public space that comes into being *in between* human beings.

For Arendt, action (*praxis*) is the highest form of human activity and needs to be sharply distinguished from work and labor. Action unlike labor and work is essentially and intrinsically political, public, communal and dialogical; action and speech always require the presence of others. Plurality is the basic human condition of action. By plurality, Arendt does not mean sheer otherness, but the distinctive individuality of human beings that is revealed and *appears* in the public realm. For her "debate constitutes the essence of politics," not the control of the legitimate means of violence, or domination. Such debate requires a public space that only springs into existence *in between* human beings and in which individuals can encounter each other as equals. Drawing on her interpretation of the Greek polis, she tells us:

Isonomy guaranteed ἰσότης, equality, but not because all
men were born or created equal, but on the contrary, because all men were by nature (φύσει) not equal, and
needed an artificial institution, the polis, which by virtue
of its νόμος would make them equal. Equality existed in
this specifically political realm, where men met one another as citizens and not as private persons. . . . The
equality of the Greek polis, its isonomy, was an attribute
of the polis and not of men, who received their equality by
virtue of citizenship, not by virtue of birth.[12]

The polis, she tells us, "properly speaking is not the city-state
in its physical location: it is the organization of the people as it
arises out of acting and speaking together, and its true space
lies between people living together for this purpose. . . ."[13]

Unlike many liberal political thinkers who think there is
a paradox or tension between equality and freedom, for Arendt
these two concepts merge. For freedom itself is primarily public freedom. It is "a tangible worldly reality, something created
by means to be enjoyed by men rather than a gift or capacity;
it [is] the man-made public space or market-place which antiq-
uity had known as the area where freedom appears and becomes visible to all."[14] In such a polis or community,
persuasion, not violence or manipulation, is the quintessence
of public life; and persuasion itself involves free open debate
among equals in which there is an attempt to clarify, test, and
purify opinions.

Several charges have frequently been brought against Arendt by her critics. She has been accused of being hopelessly
romantic, basing her understanding of political and public life
on a nostalgic conception of a "golden age" that never really
existed. Or, alternatively, it is claimed that such a conception
of public life is utopian in the face of the complexities of modern social life. Furthermore, she has been accused of being insensitive to the fact that the two most glorious examples that

she cites of the flowering of this public life—the Greek *polis* and the American Revolution—were societies in which slavery existed. But while I do think that Arendt can be criticized on many points, these criticisms miss the mark. There is very little that is nostalgic about her thinking concerning action, politics, and public life. Her primary intention is not to tell us what public life, freedom, and politics once *were*, but to clarify and recover what she takes to be a permanent possibility rooted in human natality—the capacity to begin, to initiate. She argues that in the modern world this public freedom characteristic of politics arose spontaneously and against almost all odds in the wake of revolutions, and was rarely anticipated by "professional" revolutionaries. Historically, she claims, it arose in "the French Revolution, with Jefferson in the American Revolution, in the Parisian commune, in the Russian revolutions, in the wake of revolutions in Germany and Austria at the end of World War I, finally in the Hungarian Revolution [of 1956]."[15] She saw the same phenomenon manifesting itself in the early stages of the civil rights movement and the anti-Vietnam War movement. These citizen councils "never came into being as a result of a conscious revolutionary tradition or theory but entirely spontaneously, each time as though there had never been anything of the sort before."[16] Arendt knew full well that the tragedy of the modern world is that public freedom which arises with the spontaneous formations of councils has perished every time and everywhere, destroyed either directly by the bureaucracy of the nation states or by party-machines. I have no doubt that if she were alive today, she would see the same glorious and tragic phenomenon in recent Polish events. There is a deep ambiguity running through Arendt's work concerning the prospects of the emergence of such public life in our times, but this is an ambiguity rooted in our historical situation. On the one hand, she well understood the frailty of such public life. Her interpretation of modernity with the progressive triumph of a fabricating and laboring mentality, as well as the emergence of an entirely new form of government, totalitarianism, made it increasingly improbable that such public life can arise and solve the problem of "founding," i.e., of becoming institutionalized. But on the other hand, since she understood action to be rooted in human natality—in our capacity to begin and initiate—she never gave up the hope that this potentiality might be realized again.

There *is* a utopian strain in her thinking, but it is utopian in a sense characterized by Gadamer when he tells us a "utopia is not the projection of aims for action. Rather the characteristic element of utopia is that it does not lead precisely to the moment of action, the 'setting one's hand to a job here and now.' . . . It is not primarily a project of action but a critique of the present."[17]

Concerning the accusation about her insensitivity to slavery, her elitism, and her categorial distinction between the political and the social question, one must be extremely cautious. While I do not think her divorce of politics and society will not stand up to critical examination, nevertheless her distinctions between freedom and liberation, the public and the private, politics as the area of debate and society as that of administration, are intended to highlight what is unique and distinctive about genuine public life. In what might seem to be a harsh comment, but for her was only a realistic appraisal, she declared, "Nothing, we might say today, could be more obsolete than to attempt to liberate mankind from poverty by political means; nothing could be more futile and more dangerous."[18]

It is certainly true that Arendt consistently thought that politics is only for the few—not everyone would or should engage in politics. But she never condoned the exclusion of anyone from politics. The radical thrust of thinking is evidenced when she declares:

> Not everyone wants to or has to concern himself with pub-
> lic affairs. In this fashion a self-selective process is possible
> that would draw together a true political elite in a country.
> Anyone who is not interested in public affairs will simply
> have to be satisfied with their being decided without him.
> *But each person must be given the opportunity*. (Italics added.)[19]

Coming closer to our situation, that of American public life, one can use the work of Gadamer, Habermas, and Arendt both to criticize and draw out what is most important to Dewey's vision of public life. For at times Dewey was insensitive to the distinction between the technical and the practical. He failed to appreciate how easily science and scientific method can degenerate into scientism. Dewey himself was still very much in the tradition of the Enlightenment in his expectation that when the scientific spirit became dominant in our ethical and political lives, then autonomy and freedom would become living realities. But even when all this is granted, there is a deeper message that speaks through his work. For what Dewey saw as threatened in American society was the very basis for communal life which is the substance of democracy. And he saw that what was in part responsible for this was the perversion of liberalism which tended to isolate human beings from each other. The principle of an open critical *community* in which participants share and contribute is one of the deepest themes in American philosophy, and Dewey was concerned to apply this to concrete political and social affairs. This even explains Dewey's lifelong concern with education and the school. For he thought that the school was the primary institution for the revitalization of this communal democratic ideal. Democracy for Dewey was not primarily a form of government, it was a moral ideal. "Every way of life that fails in its democracy limits the contacts, the exchanges, the communications, the interactions by which experience is steadied while it is also enlarged and enriched. The task of this release and enrichment is one that has to be carried on day by day. Since it is one that can have no end till experience itself comes to an end, the task of democracy is forever that of a creation of a freer and more humane experience in which all share and to which all contribute."[20]

As I indicated earlier, it would be misleading to suggest that Gadamer, Habermas, Arendt, and Dewey are all saying the "same thing." They are not, and an exploration of their differences can illuminate some of the complexities in the understanding of public life in our historical situation. But, nevertheless, we can also see how their differing approaches complement each other. For whether one emphasizes the need to discriminate practical reasoning and knowledge from theoretical and technical knowledge and stresses the role of genuine dialogue for cultivating such *phronesis*, or emphasizes the primacy of communicative action and discourse based upon mutual understanding of participants who are committed to seeking a rational consensus, or describes those brief and fragile moments in history when individuals come together and create a public space in which persuasion and debate rule, or stresses democracy as a moral ideal in which all share and all contribute, they collectively highlight what is required for a revitalization of authentic public life. They make us keenly aware of what needs to be confronted—developing the types of communities in which public debate and communal decision-making become genuine *practices* of citizens. They turn our attention to the substance of public life rather than its mere form. There is still an overwhelming tendency to think that politics and public life is primarily the sphere of the negotiation and conflict of competing interests. Certainly this is what "politics" has become for us today. Without denying this "reality" Gadamer, Habermas, Arendt and Dewey focus our attention on a different phenomenon that is vital for an understanding of public life. At the end of the 1960s, when Arendt sought to clarify what she meant by a new concept of the state based on a council-system, she declared:

> The councils say: We want to participate, we want to debate, we want to make our voices heard in public, and we want to have a possibility to determine the political course of our country. Since the country is too big for all of us to come together and determine our fate, we need a number of public spaces within it. The booth in which we deposit our ballots is unquestionably too small, for this booth has room for only one. The parties are completely unsuitable; there we are, most of us, nothing but the manipulated electorate. But if only ten of us are sitting around a table, each expressing his opinion, each hearing the opinions of others, then a rational formation of opinion can take place through the exchange of opinions. There too, it will become clear which one of us is best suited to present our view before the next higher council, where in turn our view will be clarified through the influence of other views, revised, or proved wrong.[21]

But although one might be inspired by this "utopian" ideal— one which Arendt herself thought had little prospect of being realized—we come to a deep paradox that needs to be confronted. Facing this paradox will bring us closer to the question of a possible role of religion in American public life.

For however much one might stress the unpredictability and spontaneous quality of individuals coming together to create such public spaces, one cannot escape the fact that such a possibility already *presupposes* a living sense of community. There must *already* exist shared understandings and experience, intersubjective meanings, commonly accepted principles, a sense of a common tradition, and those shared tacit affective ties that bind individuals together. A *polis* or a community is not something that can be *made* by some form of *techne*. Aristotle himself was profoundly aware that *phronesis* as a political virtue only makes sense if there is a living *nomos* and *ethos* that informs communal life. In this respect, there is something of a circle or spiral that is comparable to the famous hermeneutical circle. For the coming into being of such a public life which can strengthen solidarity presupposes tacit communal bonds of fellowship. But then what is to be done in a situation in which there is a breakdown of such communities, and where the very conditions of social life have the consequences of fostering such a breakdown?

We know what has been the typical modern response to this paradoxical situation. We can make, engineer, impose our collective will to form such communities. But this is precisely what cannot be done, and the attempts to do so have been disastrous.

In my opinion, the thinker who most acutely grasped this paradox, and saw it as *the* paradox of the modern world, was Hegel. Few thinkers have had a more profound sense of the meaning of ethical communal life than Hegel—what he called *Sittlichkeit*. Hegel too celebrated what he took to be the paradigm of this ideal—the Hellenic ideal. But Hegel knew full well that there was no possibility of a return to this form of immediacy. Hegel also saw that the various attempts of modern man to impose his will to create a new mediated form of spiritual community have all resulted in a series of grotesque failures—what Judith Shklar aptly calls the "moral failures of asocial man."[22] Whether there can be an overcoming (*Aufhebung*) of this situation—the emergence of a new form of mediated spiritual community—is an issue which even in Hegel is clouded in ambiguity. But where then does that leave us today?

The first point that I want to stress is the need to escape from the dangers and seductions of "totalizing" thinking—to be seduced into the illusion that the forces at work in modern society are so powerful and all-encompassing that there is no possibility of realizing the type of public life that I have been adumbrating. This is the way to despair and itself furthers a sense of our own impotence. What is so desperately needed today is to think and act more like the fox than the hedgehog. For what characterizes the modern world is not just the playing out of powerful forces which are beyond our control, but the paradoxical situation where power creates counterpower—and reveals the vulnerability of power itself; where the very forces that undermine and distort genuine communal life and public spaces also have the consequence of creating new and frequently unpredictable forms of solidarity.

The question that becomes vital is where in our society one can find the vestiges of community that might still play a role in fostering the type of public life I have been sketching. The town meeting, the neighborhood, the local community council are either destroyed or deformed in our society. Too frequently what seems to begin as the creation of a public space based on mutual recognition soon becomes another form of interest politics. It is from this perspective, that I want to raise the question of the possible role of religion in the future of American public life.

One must of course be cautious, skeptical and tentative in raising this question. What is most manifest about religious life in America is that it appears to be part of the problem rather than a solution to the problem. It suffers from the same conflicting tendencies that are exhibited in so much of our social life. On the one hand there is the strong tendency toward privatization, where it is thought that religion does not and ought not to have anything to do with public life. Religion gets assimilated to a matter of personal and private belief and taste. It takes on the coloring of the subjectivism that pervades so much of modern life. Anyone has a right to hold whatever "religious beliefs" he or she wishes as long as it doesn't "interfere" with public life. I do not want to completely mock such an idea because it can be related to the deep principle of toleration which is so much a part of our tradition. But one should not be naive about how such an ideology or attitude emasculates any possibility of religion playing a significant role in the creation of an authentic public space. On the other hand, we are all too familiar with what happens when religious groups do become "political"—they ape the interest politics that is so characteristic of American life. Many liberal thinkers have recently been deeply disturbed about the phenomenon of the Moral Majority and the ways in which other "neo-fundamentalist" religious groups are exerting political power and influence. But what is frequently neglected is how such movements themselves are in the "best" tradition of liberal interest politics. After all, we pride ourselves in thinking that any group in our society has the right to organize itself, to amass financial support, and to press its interests by the most effective strategic means that it can within the accepted legal framework. If big business, labor, or environmentalists can do this, then why not those who share similar religious or moral views? In this respect the legitimation for the formation and tactics of such groups is a reflection of the prevailing liberal ideology of politics as the bargaining and negotiation of interests. What is disturbing to many who oppose the Moral Majority is not really the legitimacy of what they are attempting to do, but their apparent success. The response of many religious leaders to the Moral Majority operates within the same framework of thinking and acting—that what is needed for those who oppose the policies and tactics of such "objectionable" groups is to organize and to advance competing interests.

I hope that nothing I have said will be interpreted as endorsing the Moral Majority, and certainly my sympathies are with those who oppose them. But the point I want to underscore is a conceptual one—that as long as one stays within the framework of thinking that where American public life is and ought to be is the bargaining among interest groups, then one has little basis for criticizing the existence and legitimacy of such groups. One must realize that the very liberal ideology which many take to be threatened by such groups as the Moral Majority is itself in part responsible for, and even provides the rationale for, the existence and tactics of such groups. What is important for my analysis is that this conception of interest politics where one fights for one's interests in the "free" marketplace underscores how *not* to think about the role of religion in American public life. For the primary issue is not one of advocating that religious groups or leaders ought to be more outspoken in taking public stands on the important political issues of the day. This can be laudable and even courageous, just as it can be offensive and objectionable. But to think about religion and public life in this manner does not really touch the heart of the matter.

Rather, I am advocating that what ought to be our primary concern is with cultivating those types of public spaces in which individuals can come together and debate; can encounter each other in the formation, clarification, and testing of opinions; where judgment, deliberation and *phronesis* can flourish; where individuals become aware of the creative power that springs up among them; where there is a tangible experience of overcoming the privatization, subjectivization, and the narcissistic tendencies so pervasive in our daily lives. And it is because—no matter how deformed and distorted—there are still the vestiges of community life and communal bonds in religious life that it might yet still play a role in the vitalization of public life. Of course there are many good reasons to be skeptical that something like this will really happen. And I do not want to suggest that it is only religious communities that can serve as a basis for a renewal of public life. But if one adopts the foxlike thinking that I am advocating—a type of thinking which is in the best American pragmatic tradition—then against the seductions of "totalizing" thinking, whether advocated by the left or the right, one must seek to take advantage of whatever opportunities arise for the creation of such public spaces. We do know, and ought not to forget, that there have been moments in our own history when religious communities have played just this role. One of the great blindnesses of prevailing theories of secularization and modernization is that they fail to make sense of the creative *potential* that still exists in forms of religious life and which has occasionally been actualized. One of the most dramatic recent examples of what I mean was manifested in the early stages of the civil rights movement. There is a danger of romanticizing and sentimentalizing just what did happen. But there is the opposite danger of forgetfulness and cynicism. For however one analyzes this movement—its origins, causes, and dynamics—no analysis is adequate unless it takes account of the creative role that religious communities played in the formation of this movement. For this was a moment in our recent history when one witnessed the interplay of religious communal life and the formation of a tangible public space. The fact that there was *already* a pre-existing sense of communal religious bonds provided many individuals with the courage, hope, and conviction to join together in public action. It illustrates what I think is becoming increasingly evident in our time—that if there is to be a renewal of public life, a communal basis for individuals coming together, it is to be found outside those great impersonal abstractions of society and state.

I would like to conclude by relating an experience that for me is paradigmatic of what I have been trying to describe. It occurred during the summer of 1964 in Hattiesburg, Mississippi. You may recall that it was a time when students, educators, ministers, and lawyers from all over the country went

to Mississippi to work with local black communities. One of
the aims of the Mississippi Summer Project was to encourage
local blacks to register, to elect delegates for the Mississippi
Freedom Democratic Party, to help initiate a process that
would lead to federal civil rights legislation. At the time I was
teaching at Yale, and several of the students planning to participate in the Project asked some of us to come to Mississippi
to support their activities. I went to Mississippi more as an observer than as a participant. The experience that I want to relate occurred in the Morningstar Baptist Church, the
headquarters for the Easton precinct of Forrest County. Many
of those who came to Mississippi that summer knew that they
would be returning to the safety of their homes at the end of
the summer. But no one knew then what would happen to the
local blacks who identified themselves with the civil rights
movement. It took an enormous amount of courage and risk to
participate. After several weeks of voter registration, the moment had arrived when it was up to the local blacks to meet
and publicly elect their representatives. That meeting was one
of the most impressive political gatherings I have ever attended. The session opened with a benediction, a keynote address, and the democratic nomination and election of a
chairperson and secretary, and proceeded to pass resolutions
and appoint delegates to attend the district meeting. As the
chairperson said, everyone was a little nervous because nothing
quite like this had ever happened in Mississippi before. As you
might imagine this gathering had something of the quality of a
religious meeting. And there were two things that deeply impressed me—that I was witnessing the creation of just one of
those public spaces that Arendt describes, and that what gave
the participants the courage, hope, and conviction to participate was informed by their religious communal bonds. It was
more than symbolic that such a meeting took place in a local
church, for it was clear that without the encouragement of the

few local pastors who identified with the civil rights movement, and the infra-structure of religious life among local blacks, the Mississippi Summer Project would never have been able to take place. We know how rare and fragile such events can be—how they occur in extraordinary circumstances when individuals experience a deep sense of crisis and injustice, and are motivated to come together. But the danger that we face today is one of forgetfulness and an overly "sophisticated" cynicism that erodes what Ernst Bloch called the principle of hope.

Recently there have been a variety of analyses of American society that portray the emergence of "psychological man" and the "culture of narcissism." The evidence in support of such a tendency seems so manifest and overwhelming that it is difficult to deny the phenomenon. But our present situation is more confused, complex, and anxious. For intertwined with this almost desperate narcissistic tendency there is an underlying anxiety. No matter how frustrated, perverted, muted, and diffused it may be, there is a longing for a genuine sense of community—not a Great Community in which our individuality is lost and submerged, but those local *communities* in which our individuality can be realized. *If* "religion" is to make a creative contribution to American public life, it is by furthering these deep aspirations, by giving them concreteness and specificity, by making them tangible public realities.

One of Arendt's favorite quotations is a passage from St. Augustine. Like a leitmotif she returns to it again and again in her writings. At the conclusion of her study of the *Origins of Totalitarianism* she tells us:

> There remains the fact that the crisis of our time and its central experience have brought forth an entirely new form of government which as a potentiality and ever-present danger is only too likely to stay with us from now on,

just as other forms of government which came about at different historical moments and rested on different fundamental experiences have stayed with mankind regardless of temporary defeats—monarchies, and republics, tyrannies, dictatorship and despotism.

But there remains also the truth that every end in history necessarily contains a new beginning; this beginning is the promise, the only "message" which the end can ever produce. Beginning, before it becomes a historical event, is the supreme capacity of man; politically, it is identical with man's freedom. *Initium ut esset homo creatus est*—"that a beginning be made man was created" said Augustine. This beginning is guaranteed by each new birth; it is indeed every man.[23]

Notes

1. Hans-Georg Gadamer, "Hermeneutics and Social Science," *Cultural Hermeneutics* 2 (1975), 312.

2. Jürgen Habermas, *Theory and Practice* (Boston: Beacon Press, 1973), p. 255.

3. Hannah Arendt, *The Human Condition* (Chicago: University of Chicago Press, 1958), p. 279.

4. Recent scholarship has shown that Weber's conceptions of rationality and rationalization processes in society are far more complex and subtle than is stated here. I am limiting myself in this context to *one* strain in his thinking that has been extremely influential. For a comprehensive analysis of Weber's understanding of rationality see Wolfgang Schluchter, *The Rise of Western Rationalism* (Berkeley: University of California Press, 1981).

5. Jürgen Habermas, *Toward a Rational Society* (Boston: Beacon Press, 1970), p. 103.

6. Gadamer, "Hermeneutics and Social Science," p. 316.

7. Hans-Georg Gadamer, "The Problem of Historical Consciousness," in Paul Rabinow and William S. Sullivan, eds., *Interpretative Social Science: A Reader* (Berkeley: University of California Press, 1979), p. 107. This essay, especially in "The Hermeneutical Problem and Aristotle's Ethics," provides a succinct statement of Gadamer's appropriation of *phronesis*. See also *Reason in the Age of Science* (Cambridge, Mass.: M.I.T. Press, 1981) for a further development of the fusion of hermeneutics and praxis.

8. Hans-Georg Gadamer, *Truth and Method* (New York: Seabury Press, 1975), p. 347.

9. Gadamer, *Reason in the Age of Science*, p. 87.

10. Jürgen Habermas, *Communication and the Evolution of Society* (Boston: Beacon Press, 1979), p. 118. The fullest statement of Habermas' theory of communicative action has recently been published in two volumes as *Theorie des Kommunikativen Handelns* (Frankfurt: Suhrkamp Verlag, 1981). Volume I is available in English translation as *The Theory of Communicative Action: Reason and the Rationalization of Society* (Boston: Beacon Press, 1984).

11. Hannah Arendt, "Truth and Politics," in *Between Past and Future* (New York: Viking Press, 1961).

12. Hannah Arendt, *On Revolution* (New York: Viking Press, 1963), p. 23.

13. Arendt, *The Human Condition*.

14. Arendt, *On Revolution*, p. 120.

15. Hannah Arendt, *Crises of the Republic* (New York: Harcourt Brace Jovanovich, 1972), p. 230.

16. *Ibid.*

17. Gadamer, *Reason in the Age of Science*, p. 80.

18. Arendt, *On Revolution*, p. 110.

19. Arendt, *Crises of the Republic*, p. 233.

20. John Dewey, "Creative Democracy—The Task Before Us," in Max Fisch, ed., *Classic American Philosophers* (New York: Appleton-Century-Crofts, 1951), p. 394.

21. Arendt, *Crises of the Republic*, p. 233.

22. Judith Shklar, *Freedom and Independence* (Cambridge, Mass.: Harvard University Press, 1976). See chapter 3, "The Moral

Failures of Asocial Men." See also Charles Taylor's analysis of this paradox in *Hegel and Modern Society* (Cambridge: Cambridge University Press, 1979).

23. Hannah Arendt, *The Origins of Totalitarianism* (New York: Viking Press, 1958), p. 478.

Religious Sensibility and the Reconstruction of Public Life: Prospectus for a New America

Douglas Sturm

Shine, Perishing Republic

While this America settles in the mould of its vulgarity,
    heavily thickening to empire,
And protest, only a bubble in the molten mass, pops
    and sighs out, and the mass hardens,

I sadly smiling remember that the flower fades to make
    fruit, the fruit rots to make earth.

. . . .

And boys, be in nothing so moderate as in love of man,
    a clever servant, insufferable master.
There is the trap that catches noblest spirits, that caught
    —they say—God, when he walked the earth.[1]

AS THE POETS KNOW SO WELL, the ambiguities of politics
are surpassed only by the ambiguities of religion—or is it the

53

other way around? In either case, so accustomed have we become to the hermeneutics of suspicion, we have good reason to despair of both these enterprises. That is what makes our assigned charge so difficult. We are to develop agenda for inquiry into religion and the future of public life in America. Difficult as the charge is, its import cannot be gainsaid, for our destiny, at least in the historical realm, may well rest on the character of our religious insight and political action.

To those with sophistication in current studies in theology and political theory, we need not bother with a lengthy apology about connections. We can, perhaps, accept as a premise Alexis de Tocqueville's assertion:

> Every religion has some political opinion linked to it by affinity. The spirit of man, left to follow its bent, will regulate political society and the City of God in uniform fashion; it will, if I dare put it so, seek to *harmonize* earth with heaven.[2]

There is an interplay, however it is to be construed exactly, between social order and social consciousness, and religious sensibility is a dimension of social consciousness.

> The religious conception of reality is the basic level of social consciousness in several senses. Religion represents the most general expression of the beliefs that nourish and unify the several branches of a type of social consciousness. It exhibits the characteristics of social consciousness in their purest and most complete form. And it is always involved, more or less directly, in every change of social ideals and beliefs. Thus, the religious consciousness deals with the whole of experience.[3]

To pose the issue of the *future* of public life in America seems to assume two things. First, it is to assume that public life is not a given. However indomitable its current structures appear, it is a construction. It is a work never fully accomplished. It is an enactment. By what we are, by what we do, and by what we say, we are engaged in a process of its formation or reformation. Only thus can we speak meaningfully of a future.

Second, it is to assume that the current condition of public life is unsatisfactory. As Vincent Harding has observed,

> I see all of America as a kind of contested territory. The old definitions and the old visions of what America is and ought to be are passing away. They have, in many cases, been crashed aside by the events especially of the past 25 to 30 years. At this moment new definitions, new visions, new understandings are in the throes of construction and creation. . . . We must try to create and project a courageous vision of what ought to be, of what *must* be, not only for the humanizing of America, but also for the safety of the world.[4]

Many there are who declare we are in a state of crisis whether it be a "legitimation crisis" (Habermas),[5] the "decline of business civilization" (Heilbroner),[6] a movement "beyond liberalism" (Kariel),[7] the "twilight of authority" (Nisbet),[8] or the "twilight of capitalism" (Harrington).[9]

The assumption of crisis is, of course, as much a question as it is an assumption. There *is* a sense of malaise, serious malaise, that pervades many segments of American society. But what are the roots of that malaise? How are we to name the crisis? Naming the crisis, I would propose, is a preliminary, yet paramount question for our inquiry.

The naming of a crisis, I suggest, is ultimately an expression of religious sensibility. In medicine, a crisis is a turning point, a moment of life or death. In drama, a crisis is a decisive event in the development of the protagonist's story, an event determinative of the protagonist's future. In public life, a crisis, in the strict sense, is a time of potentially radical social change. It is a time portending some transformation of the human condition. It marks a transition in historical epoch. It signifies the beginnings of a new chapter in the "biography of the gods."[10]

Alfred North Whitehead has noted that "the topic of religion is individuality in community."[11] One way to construe historical epochs is the manner in which "individuality in community" is embodied in social order and social consciousness. In simplified form, the transition from the medieval to the modern world is the shift from a principle of organic hierarchy to a principle of individualism.[12]

American society has been organized, according to recurrently stated intentions, to honor the principle of individualism. The liberty of the individual has been the "prospective image"[13] of the New World. That principle constitutes the heart of American liberalism. But American liberalism has soured. In part it has soured because of its exclusiveness. Significant populations within the American community have yet, despite two hundred years of the democratic experiment, to experience the benefits of its promise. Furthermore it has soured because of its perverse use to justify concentrations of wealth and power that redound not to the freedom of the human spirit, but to the perpetuation of control, witting or unwitting, by an elite.[14]

The crisis which gives rise to concern for the future of American public life is centered in the inability of the principle of individualism as it has been embodied in the institutions and consciousness of American society to ground and to support a genuinely public life as needed at this point of history.

An alternative that is not without roots in the American experience is a principle of internal relations. Here I make appeal to the tradition of process thought in its philosophical and theological expressions. According to this principle of internal relations, everything in the universe is conjoined with everything else in a continuous process of becoming. Each entity has its own integrity, yet stands in a kind of essential relationship with all other entities. The universe is self-transcending. It is always to some degree and in some sense a moving beyond.[15] In Whitehead's language,

> The actual world, the world of experiencing, and of thinking, and of physical activity, is a community of many diverse entities; and these entities contribute to, or derogate from, the common value of the total community. At the same time, these actual entities are, for themselves, their own value, individual and separable. They add to the common stock and yet they suffer alone. The world is a scene of solitariness in community.[16]

Within this metaphysic, religious sensibility is responsiveness to the full context of one's existence, to its limitations and its possibilities, and to the burden of responsibility one bears for its enrichment or degradation. God is "that sensitive nature within the full context of nature, winning the creative passage for qualitative attainment."[17] The principle of internal relations can be understood as a conceptual rendition of the covenantal tradition, a not unimportant strain in American history.

In political thought, this principle of internal relations is communitarian. As such it provides a ground for preserving what is of value in the liberal tradition, but casts it in a new framework which, I would argue, is more adequate to the needs of our time.

From this perspective I offer six topics for inquiry: (1) the absence, (2) the ground, (3) the meaning, (4) the problem, (5) the principles, and (6) the study of public life.

1. THE ABSENCE OF PUBLIC LIFE:
ISOLATION VERSUS PARTICIPATION

Concern has long been expressed over the extent and depth of political alienation in American society, measured in some cases by election statistics. But serious doubt has been voiced for several decades over whether a genuinely public life is at all possible in modern times. There are, it has been argued, features central to the character of modern culture that militate against the formation and maintenance of an effective polis.

A case in point is John Dewey's argument, formulated over fifty years ago, that there has been an "eclipse of the public."[18] In Dewey's pragmatic conception, a public is a group of persons mobilized for action because it suffers from the indirect consequences of a transaction effected by other parties. Within the early years of the American republic, the mobilization of such groups was an easy matter because the society was organized around small local centers. But social conditions have been totally transformed by the growth of modern commerce and technology. The town meeting is virtually a thing of the past. "The machine age has so enormously expanded, multiplied, intensified and complicated the scope of the indirect consequences, have [sic] formed such immense and consolidated unions in action, on an impersonal rather than a community basis, that the resultant public cannot identify and distinguish itself."[19] Dewey cites the First World War as a case of the enormity of the problem. What might he say today? He also notes the contortions by which the principle of individualism has become a justification for its very antithesis.

At the outset, it was held by "progressives," by those who were protesting against the inherited regime of rules of law and administration. Vested interests, on the contrary, were mainly in favor of the old status. Today the industrial-property regime being established, the doctrine is the intellectual bulwark of the standpatter and reactionary. He it is that now wants to be left alone, and who utters the war-cry of liberty for private industry, thrift, contract and their pecuniary fruit.[20]

In a vivid interpretation of our political condition shortly following World War II, Hannah Arendt insists that an enduring public realm is possible only where grounded in an authoritative tradition which provides the expectations, thus the social space in which and through which a people might act in concert. But critique of traditionality and loss of authority are central features of the modern mind before which all inheritances are subject to skeptical analysis. The ultimate break with tradition in the realm of the practical was effected by totalitarianism to which nothing is sacred. Given the full force of modernity, each individual remains in isolation, susceptible to the sufferings of meaninglessness. Save for rare moments, moments of revolution or resistance, where persons may be thrust temporarily into common action, the public realm—the realm of practical freedom—is a mirage.[21]

Yet even during the 1960s, a decade of significant resistance activity, the absence of an authentic public realm was noted. Robert J. Pranger argues that a citizen's primary task is to participate in the doing of public business, but in the modern Western world a politics of participation has given way to a politics of power. Not participation but domination characterizes the American political scene. The bureaucratization of organizational life has sharply delimited areas of citizen engagement. Resistance movements are efforts merely to counter power with power. The reduction of the public realm to a point of insignificance has resulted in the "eclipse of citizenship."[22]

More recently, Richard Sennett has announced the "fall of public man."[23] Sennett's version is that the dislocations of life produced by capitalism have given rise to an ideology of intimacy. The social distance and psychological courage needed for public action have become identified with the impersonality and dehumanizing effects of capitalist structures, and are eschewed for the warmth of immediate relations. Even within the political realm, matters of personality take precedence over issues of policy. Civility, an attitude which enables persons to engage in transactions with others without close acquaintanceship, has been shunted aside for kinship resulting in a trend toward the tyranny of localism and tribalization. The exaltation of personal warmth as a reaction against the dissociative tendencies of industrial capitalism signals the end of public culture.

As Thomas Luckmann[24] has so ingeniously argued, a similar phenomenon has occurred in the religious sphere. Whereas, in previous periods of history, religion served to provide a sacred cosmos diffused throughout and legitimating all aspects of the social structure, a radical transformation has occurred in the age of industrialization. Institutions are legitimated not by an encompassing religious myth, but by norms of functional rationality. Specialized areas of life have become separated from each other. Individuals still seek out a sacred cosmos, but no single official model is available. Religion has thus become privatized, individualized, in effect, "invisible." That is the new form of religion in modern times. A radical bifurcation has been created between the inner religious world and the world of social interaction.

Thus even as the public sphere has become eclipsed given features of modern life—the force of modern technology, the loss of traditionality, the politics of power and domination, and the escape to intimacy—so religion seems to have lost its public significance.

But has it? The complaint of political theology is that it has not. To be sure, religion has taken a subjective turn. Thus existentialist theology, concerned with the dehumanizing structures of modern industrial society, has pointed to the intensely personal divine-human encounter as the source of meaning and fulfillment. The I-Thou relationship between God and the individual transcends, it is claimed, the processes and patterns of historical life. But, the political theologians shrewdly charge, the privatization of the religious encounter reflects and thereby reinforces the individualism of bourgeois ideology. Indirectly it supports the inhumane effects of bourgeois institutions by failing to challenge them for what they are. The argument of political theology is that the intended privatization of religion is a deception because of the solidary character of reality. Personalized religion is necessarily of public significance, but in a negative, if not ultimately a perverse, way.[25]

2. THE GROUND OF PUBLIC LIFE: ATOMISM VERSUS CONTEXTUALISM

Questions of the ground and of the meaning of public life are intertwined. They may not, in the final analysis, be separable. But, to reinforce my general theme, I shall for the moment separate them. The question of ground asks about roots or origins. At its most basic level it is an issue of cosmology. It is concerned with the setting of public life. The question of meaning, on the other hand, asks about the structure of public life as such. It is concerned with the "orienting concept"[26] or categorical definition of politics.

Classical political philosophy, as it appears, for instance, in Aristotle and Thomas Aquinas, is expressive of a fundamental understanding of the character of the world. The Aristotelian and Thomistic approaches to political life cannot be adequately comprehended apart from a teleological view of nature. Public life is intrinsic to the maturation of the human species.

The emergence of the modern world, however, is marked with a different vision of the character of the world and therefore of the beginnings of public life. Therein lies the genius of Thomas Hobbes. His "politics of motion"[27] gave voice to the new vision in a clear and direct manner. But the new vision has become more than merely a theory debated by philosophers. It has come, declares Roberto Unger, to "occupy a central place in our everyday thinking as well as in the specialized branches of social study."[28] It is the "unreflective view of society" that is generally presupposed and acted upon throughout liberal culture. More pointedly, Frank M. Coleman has argued "that American constitutional tradition is the product of a revolutionary movement in political thought whose directions and nature are embodied in Hobbes's major works and that Hobbes, not Locke, is the parent source of American constitutional philosophy."[29]

In C.B. MacPherson's telling phrase, the central assumption of the new vision is "possessive individualism."[30] Given that assumption, public life is not primary to human existence. It is not intrinsic to the development of the human species. It is an artifice. It has a remedial function to perform. Behind public life stands the "state of nature." "The State of Nature," declares Coleman, "is the literacy vehicle employed by Hobbes to advance the claims of modern egoism."[31] As such, it betrays what human beings are conceived to be in their most pristine condition. They are individuals in action—atoms in motion—reaching out to grasp whatever is pleasing to them. They are propelled by self-interest. The image is that of market society.

But, given a relative scarcity of resources, persons are seized in a competitive struggle which, in its extremity, becomes a war of all against all. Without the introduction of some principle of order, without, that is to say, the restraints of public life, existence would be "solitary, poor, nasty, brutish, and short."[32]

Public life is thus grounded in the limitations and frustrations of the state of nature. The social contract through which persons consent to be governed is a compact of convenience. It may be functionally necessary. But it is an intrusion into the primary activity of life. Political order is secondary to economic pursuit. Politics is alien to one's most fundamental inclinations. It goes against the grain of personal desire.

But as new occasions teach new duties, so shifting historical conditions provoke new imageries of thought and action. In William Ernest Hocking's formulation, we are now, on the far side of the twentieth century, at a point of "passing beyond modernity,"[33] of moving toward a principle of intersubjectivity. That same sense underlies John MacMurray's thesis "the the Self is constituted by its relation to the Other; that it has its being in its relationships; and that this relationship is necessarily personal."[34] More generally, a change is discernible from an atomistic to a contextualist cosmology which alters the setting of public life. The self is not the subjective or isolated ego, but person in relation. Bernard Eugene Meland has pointed to developments in the natural and social sciences tending toward a contextualist view of reality in general and a holistic understanding of humanity in particular. Within this understanding, both individuation and relatedness are essential features of existence.

> The integrity and authenticity of the person present one aspect; the claims of our communal ground present another. These are not antithetical aspects merely, for their occurrence simultaneously in any society and their interaction upon one another assures a depth of freedom and

solidarity which is spiritually greater in sensitivity and creative power than either individualism or communalism taken singly.[35]

In John MacMurray's rendition, this is an understanding of human existence that lies at the very heart of religious sensibilities, for the function of religion is "to create, maintain, and deepen the community of persons and to extend it without limit, by the transformation of negative motives and by eliminating the dominance of fear in human relations."[36] In MacMurray's argument, religion, in its purest and truest form, is the celebration of communion through worship of the One in relation to whom all entities are cherished.

The cosmology of contextualism provides a new setting for reflection about and the practice of public life. From this perspective, the initiating impulse of public life is not primarily to construct conditions for the maturation of a prescribed and pre-given set of human potentialities. Nor is it to construct defenses to delimit the war of all against all. It is instead to give deliberative expression to the interactive processes that constitute the stuff of life in such a way to enhance the experience of each one. To be sure, regardless of the originating vision of public life, perversion is possible. But without an originating vision, perversion is unrecognizable. The ground of public life is the foundation for constructing the meaning of public life.

3.

THE MEANING OF PUBLIC LIFE: PRIVATE INTEREST VERSUS SUSTAINING COMMUNITY

If our concern is with the future of public life in America, we must have some sense of what it means to speak about "public life." We must be able to specify, however generally, what typifies the public, presumably as distinguished from the private, side of our existence. Definitions of this kind are notoriously elusive. But they are also indispensable and revealing. Their indispensability was addressed some years ago by David Easton in his significant "inquiry into the state of political science."[37] Without an "orienting concept," any inquiry remains diffuse and unfocused. But definitions are also revealing. They disclose a way of thinking and a way of acting. They bear the risk of ideological bias.

"Each generation," Easton asserts, "redefines its own image of political science, with greater insight, one might hope, as our understanding of political life increases."[38] Maybe, however, understanding of political life is not simply cumulative. Whatever the reasons are for the paradigm shifts in history, they seem not to be merely the functions of increased knowledge. Insight and understanding are bounded in complex ways, but, of the two, insight, I suspect, occupies the place of priority. Whether the insight of one generation is greater than another may depend on how responsive it is to the needs of the time.

Harold Lasswell's presentation of politics as "who gets what, when, how"[39] was a stroke of insight. In this presentation, public life is discerned as transactions of influence and power. Institutional forms, carefully designed in constitutional documents and basic policies, may or may not represent actual happenings. But public life is a matter of actual happenings. And, on that level, individuals and groups jockey with each other for advantage. This movement is characteristic of both domestic and international politics. There are winners and there are losers. Yet the process is perpetual and the sides change. Governments function as dominant places of exchange. Their form, their procedures, and their results betray the transactional processes in which the whole of society is engaged. The lesson to any group that feels left out is to organize.

Underlying this rendition of the meaning of public life, so Henry S. Kariel argues, is a myth—the "Myth of the Liberal Enlightenment."

> The myth to which the Americans keep returning as they sense themselves to be under pressure can be seen in its most explicit form in the writing of its originators—that is, in the political theory of eighteenth-century English liberalism. Determined to defend a new regime in opposition to repressive feudal institutions, Thomas Hobbes, John Locke, Adam Smith, and James Madison were *compelled* to elucidate, and they did so unashamedly. They frankly proclaimed that a society was wanted in which everybody would be committed to the rational pursuit of self-interest. They elaborately announced their faith in salvation through private endeavor.[40]

Under the spell of this "myth" government is conceived to have two purposes: to protect private interest and to defend the society as a whole from external (and inner subversive) threats. Larger questions about the overall quality of the common life, the goals of human existence, the justifiability of prevailing organizational patterns are bracketed as not proper subjects for public debate and determination. They are matters reserved, it is presumed, for individuals to decide in the privacy of their homes, their religious communities and their local associations.

The almost paradoxical twist is that, over the course of time, "private interests" have come to mean the interests not of individuals and small local associations, but of corporate enterprise. "Under the aegis of the Myth of Liberalism, corporate business has emerged as virtually sovereign in America. Elite-governed industrial and financial giants have become the effective integrators of conflicting interests; they have emerged

as the all-absorbing determinants of opportunities for gener-
ating options for the whole of society."[41]

Even within the context of corporate America, political
processes are conceived as consisting in transactional relations,
with government assigned the role of conflict-management.[42]
Ultimately, however, such an understanding of the meaning
of public fails: "If public order is presented with some new and
severe trial, requiring a more creative use of public authority,
the sovereign will be incapable of action."[43] Coleman instances
four such trials currently confronting American public life:
structural unemployment, pollution and energy use, urban de-
cay, and criminal recidivism.[44] Transactional politics cannot
deal adequately with pervasive problems of public life.

An alternative understanding of the function of the political process was stated by A.D. Lindsay: "to serve the community, to remove the disharmonies which threaten its
common life and to make it more a community."[45] To Lindsay,
the political ideal was a form of democracy in which principles
of equality and liberty are infused and informed by the religious sensibility of love.[46] Sebastian de Grazia also discerns the
conformity of the political and the religious impulse:

> Those responsible for knowledge of the connectedness of
> things within the community and the order of them to-
> ward the highest good are the statesman and the theolo-
> gian. . . . The communities they represent, the political
> and the religious communities or the great community,
> take in all of man's life. Theirs is the task of raising and
> holding before men's eyes the vision of the ideal commu-
> nity.[47]

Politics so construed is not simply "who gets what, when,
how." It is more importantly an explicit manifestation of the
quality of our living together. The purpose of public life is to
pursue ways and means of improving that quality. It is to cre-

ate and to sustain those relationships in which the actions of each enhance the life of all. On those grounds, de Grazia is critical of the competitive principle of the business ideology.[48] In effect, de Grazia insists that economic activity is to be made subservient to political and religious considerations.[49]

While public life cannot and should not ignore issues of private interest, its more critical function at this juncture of history is with issues of "belonging," for, in Philip Hefner's judgment:

> Today we have a renewed sense of (1) our belonging to our fellow human beings, across all barriers—racial, sexual, economic, geographical, national, and age; (2) our belonging to the ecosystem of which we are a part, the natural environment which is the womb of our emergence and the support system for everything human; and (3) our belonging to the matrix of evolutionary development out of which our total ecosystem has unfolded.[50]

Hefner's statement may be but a form of whistling in the dark. I would, however, prefer to consider it an enlightening insight showing up the darkness of our common life for what it is.

4. THE PROBLEM OF PUBLIC LIFE: ALLOCATION VERSUS ALIENATION

Religious movements and political processes have in common a sense of something wrong with the world. This sense is particularly keen in the religious sphere. Indeed, the realism of religion is found in what John Smith calls its "dark side":

> All religions of scope and depth are filled with a clear sense of the negative judgment on existence. Life as it exists— the life of the "natural" man—is distorted; it is not as it

ought to be because it harbors within itself some flaw or deep need that has to be met with and overcome before we can speak confidently of the triumph of the ideal. Far from being the complacent celebration of a transcendent goodness existing above and beyond historical life, the religious perspective forces us to acknowledge the reality of evil and of some deep-seated obstacle that stands between us as we naturally exist and the attainment of the ideal.[51]

The political world, however, is not without its own moments of darkness which are provocative of exceptional response. In a striking parallel, Hannah Arendt associates specifically public action with religious miracle. Significant acts of public initiative like the miracles reported in the Gospels are responses to instances of dire need. As such, they are extraordinary expressions of freedom. They are "interruptions of some natural series of events, of some automatic process, in whose context they constitute the wholly unexpected."[52] "And the more heavily the scales are weighted in favor of disaster, the more miraculous will the deed done in freedom appear; for it is disaster, not salvation, which always happens automatically and therefore must appear to be irresistable."[53]

Yet even in the more ordinary run of events, political processes are motivated by some feeling of need. In John Dewey's interpretation, for instance, a public is called into being when a people suffers the consequences of actions they have not themselves directly initiated.[54] A public is a reactive group seeking to gain control over the quality of its life. There is no public life with provocation.

The liberal tradition is devoid of the tragic sense of life. But it does have means of ascertaining when something has gone wrong and when corrective action is needed. In its utilitarian form, its measure is the greatest happiness principle. Given that measure, its concern is with the felt pleasures and pains of life as these are registered in the political process by groups mobilized to press their interests. Intensity of protest backed with organized power is the mark of a political problem. That is what signals the need for readjustment in the distribution of social and economic benefits.

In its human rights form, the liberal tradition possesses a more durable and fixed standard of need. At least in principle, any violation of human rights should provoke corrective public action even in the absence of organized protest. Thus the judicial process is presumed available to protect the rights of each and every individual citizen however lowly in social status and however lacking in political power. The Bill of Rights is a promise of benefits that belong to everyone irrespective of utilitarian calculus. As such it is a gauge of public wrongs, a means of ascertaining when something has gone wrong and demands public response.

While the utility principle and the human rights principle present somewhat different versions of the problem of public life, in a sense they are the same. From both perspectives, the problem is one of allocating benefits to individuals and groups. Both tend to treat the wrongs of public life in piecemeal fashion. Both are blind to the more deep-seated and systemic distortions that permeate modern life. Neither perspective is searching enough to penetrate to the central problem of our time, the problem of structural alienation.

By alienation I mean a negative form of belonging. Sometimes the term is taken to designate psychological and social distancing, the separation of being from being. But in this context I take alienation to a point to a special kind of relationship, a relationship which is inherently contradictory. It is a relationship in which a people are caught in a pattern of activity that goes contrary to that people's own good. It is an institutional pattern in which a people suffers from the pernicious consequences of its own life-activity. It is, to use a literary image, a social form of the Frankenstein, a creation that turns back upon its creator.

The self, declares Roberto Unger, consists in three relationships—to nature, to others, and to self. The good for the self is contingent on the quality of these relationships. Where those relationships are mutually enhancing, the good for the self is realized. But the problem of public life in our times is that those relationships are mutually destructive. Thus we confront an ecological crisis, a social crisis, and an economic crisis which, in their conjunction, constitute a dire threat to human existence. Some argue that these crises, serious though they be, are far overshadowed by the "exterminism" of the nuclear weapons crisis.[55] The curiosity is that all these crises are of human making. And they persist and intensify because of institutional forms and policies we continue to support and to reinforce. Neither the utilitarian calculus nor the resolution of conflicts over rights—at least as these procedures have been carried on heretofore—will do to confront the current problem of public life.

Nothing less than a radical transformation of our common life will blunt the self-destructive drive of current policies and practices in the ecological sphere. John Cobb calls for an "ecological asceticism" that would affect forms of transportation, residential patterns, industrial strategies, military technology, land use, energy usage, waste disposal, and population control.[56] But such a change in style of life rests on the emergence of new forms of philosophical understanding and religious commitment, for in the absence of an altered state of mind the urgency of institutional revision cannot even be discerned.

The same approach applies to the social crisis. The persistence and virulence of racism and sexism in American culture show the full force of the thesis. Despite valiant efforts over decades to overcome these self-induced diseases of the human spirit through traditional forms of political pressure and judicial process, the results have been peripheral. The cultural and institutional hegemony of the white male is a seemingly ineluctable datum of American society and constitutes a central feature of the problem of public life from which, though they know it not, even white males suffer.[57] Only through an understanding that each of us essentially belongs to the other can the problem be adequately perceived.

In Michael Harrington's interpretation, the economic crisis is similarly of a structural character. Unemployment, inflation, and poverty derive from the nation's pattern of investment which is governed by the priorities of the corporate world. "There is no doubt," he writes, "that the corporate domination of the economy and the attendant ideological assumption that private control of investment yields a maximum public happiness are basic causes of the current crisis."[58] The key to solution is "the democratization of the investment function."[59] Unless the community can gain control over the productive process to direct its energies toward the enhancement of the community and of the ecosphere, persons will simply continue to participate in and contribute to a system that contradicts their own best interests. The issue is how to subordinate the economy to public control.

5. THE PRINCIPLES OF PUBLIC LIFE: COMPROMISE VERSUS JUSTICE AND COMMON GOOD

There is merit to the slogan that politics is the art of compromise. Where society is conceived as an arena in which individuals engage in a process of give-and-take, where the magnitude of things to be given-and-taken is limited, and where stability of relations is favored, compromise is a principled form of interaction. In the lexicon of American politics, compromise is a positively charged word. "Essentially, for us, compromise means that politically interested groups or parties have contended, seriously but not fatally, in a relatively free market with their various strengths of argument and social power in order to reach a transient settlement that is, for a time, acceptable to most, though maximally pleasing to none."[60] As such, compromise is central to the ethics of American public life.

> "Compromise" is at least on the edge of being a virtue in Anglo-Saxon discourse. It does not solve the world's problems once and for all, but it at least provides for the world's ongoingness. It permits us to rise the morning after knowing that certain of our complaints have been met, that the garbage will be taken, that the police will not strike, that a minority group will not reach a boiling point. Politics, is, after all, the art of the possible; compromise might seem to be its code of manners. Compromise avoids disgrace, and it may reconcile.[61]

A distinction should perhaps be drawn, however, between conflicting *interests* and conflicting *principles*.[62] Where there are conflicting interests and all pertinent parties share a concern for the duration of the general process of social interchange, compromise is an acceptable norm. Compromise is more difficult and less acceptable where principles are at stake. Firmly held political ideologies and deeply felt religious beliefs are not easily qualified when threatened by countervailing claims. The force of American liberalism, on the other hand, has been to soften the edges of ideologies and creeds. The principle of individualism subjectivizes beliefs. Principles become interests and compromise becomes possible if not mandatory between political parties and religious groups. That is the force of Robert Paul Wolff's dictum: "The genius of American politics is its ability to treat even matters of principle as though they are conflicts of interest."[63] The liberal form of religious tolerance is a supreme instance of the results of that trend. The "balancing test" in the judicial process is another case of the same tendency. The sanction for the rule of compromise is the suspicion that, in its absence, everyone loses. The more sophisticated form of the rule is the utilitarian calculus.

But, as already noted, the utilitarian calculus as applied in America has not served us well. Procedures for striking a compromise have not been so benign as pretended. They have taken the form of what Martin P. Golding euphemistically calls "offensive bargaining": "In offensive bargaining the positions of the parties are almost as asymmetrical as can be. One side is powerful, the other weak; one side has a large threat potential, the other's is small."[64] What Golding calls "offensive bargaining" might more appropriately be labeled exploitation or oppression. From a sacramental view of reality, it is sacrilege or profanation. In the vocabulary of the ethical tradition, it is injustice or dehumanization. Its forms in American public life are legion as those who are black, female, native American, unemployed, of Hispanic or Oriental origin can testify.[65]

When the powerless are brought to the bargaining table, they may have more to gain than to lose, but the odds are that they will not gain what is needful for full participation in the public life of the nation. That is the point of those who rightly claim that compromise should give way to justice as the paramount principle of politics.[66] The centrality of the principle of justice has long been recognized in the Western religious tradition from the ancient utterances of the Hebrew prophets (Amos) to the modern reconstructions of neo-Thomism (Maritain),[67] and political theology (Moltmann).[68]

Precise meanings of justice vary.[69] But whether justice is understood as liberty (Nozick),[70] equality (Honore),[71] reciprocity (Gould),[72] or wisdom (Strauss),[73] it signifies respect for the intrinsic dignity of human existence. It is a judgment against offensive bargaining. It is a declaration that some forms of compromise are intolerable. It is a directive that every person should be granted those rights and resources needed for effective participation in public life. Justice, as I would understand it in the context of modern industrial society, mandates a form of "affirmative constitutionalism"[74] for all large organizational structures, political and economic.[75] As Carl J. Friedrich has argued, the roots of Western constitutionalism have their beginnings and find their sustenance in the Hebraic-Christian idea of transcendent justice.[76]

Justice is a distributive principle. As such, it is only one side of the coin of political ethics. The other side—perhaps at this juncture of history the more prominent side—is an aggregative (or, better, a holistic) principle, the common good.[77]

Robert Bellah distinguishes three forms of political pluralism, one of which demonstrates the force and character of this principle. Liberal pluralism is atomistic; it subverts all non-contractual solidarities. Romantic pluralism is tribalistic; it reinforces the love of one's own. But there is also a "pluralism open to transcendence":

> It will be a pluralism that (1) is in search of universality while recognizing that every universal is apprehended only in particularity and concreteness; (2) can assert the validity of one's own and the right not to have that trampled on by anyone else; and (3) is developed in the context of the assertion of the good of the whole, not just the good of the national whole, but the good of the global whole.[78]

The common good is the good of the whole which is "derivative from the inter-relations of its component individuals, and also necessary for the existence of each of these individuals."[79] On the level of small groups, the common good is the goodness of friendship. On a political level, it is the goodness

of there being a public at all. On still a third level, it is the goodness of the entire "biotic pyramid."[80] In an image presented by
Scott Buchanan,

> The purpose of the city in the valley would be the en-
> hancement of nature including human nature in the valley.
> Human beings would no longer be exploiting nature or
> themselves. They would be free citizens in a constitutional
> kingdom of nature.[81]

The common good, to be sure, does not always rest easily
with the demands of justice. There are times when, for the sake
of the community, the sacrificial commitment of the individual
or of a group is demanded. In Daniel Maguire's depiction,

> The common good . . . is a descriptive term that carries
> normative clout. It describes that which meets the needs
> of community existence and it implies that you ought to
> think of those needs when assessing your personal goals.
> The term "common good" implies a dialectic between
> what might suit your narrowly personal needs and the req-
> uisites of a common life. The use of the term seems to im-
> port that individual good and community good cannot be
> conflated but must coexist in a perpetual bargaining pos-
> ture.[82]

Yet, it must be insisted, justice and common good are not
contradictory principles of public life. Neither is possible in
the absence of the other. Both are expressive of religious sensibility as framed by Alfred North Whitehead:

> The moment of religious consciousness starts from self-
> valuation, but it broadens into the concept of the world as
> a realm of adjusted values, mutually intensifying or mu-
> tually destructive. . . . Religion is world-loyalty.[83]

6. THE STUDY OF PUBLIC LIFE:
EMPIRICAL ANALYSIS VERSUS DIALOGICAL
HOLISM

Modern political analysis was launched as a distinct discipline in America near the end of the nineteenth century.[84] Behavioralism is its culmination. The analytic principle, which is a particular form of individualism, is its guiding spirit.[85] Analysis means the separation of things into parts. Analysis divides, distinguishes, brackets, sorts out in order to understand. It supposes that separation results in clarification. It favors the qualities of speciality, objectivity, neutrality, and predictability.

According to Heinz Eulau,

> A science of politics which deserves its name must build from the bottom up by asking simple questions that can, in principle, be answered; it cannot be built from the top down by asking questions that, one has reason to suspect, cannot be answered at all, at least by the methods of science. An empirical discipline is built by the slow, modest, and piecemeal cumulation of relevant theories and data. The great issues of politics, such as the conditions and consequences of freedom, justice, or authority, are admittedly significant topics, but they are topics compounded with a strong dose of metaphysical discourse. I don't think they are beyond the reach of behavioral investigation, but before they can be tackled, the groundwork must be laid.[86]

Specialization is the institutional form of the analytic principle, a form whose power is manifest in the growth of the knowledge industry: the consulting firm, the public opinion center, the think-tank, the technical expert.

The technical expert is, presumably, objective and neutral. Both of these qualities entail a bracketing. Objectivity entails bracketing personal judgments and hunches in order to represent the world for what it is; it assumes the world is external to oneself. Neutrality entails bracketing evaluation and assessment in order to let the bare facts be what they are; it assumes that values are not grounded in factuality but are imposed on the world as a matter of personal orientation. Thus the analytic principle effects a radical dualism of Manichaean proportions between objectivity and subjectivity and between factuality and evaluation.

In addition, the analytic principle presses toward the formulation of propositions enabling one to predict the course of events at least within the limits of probability and—curiously—gives rise to the hope one may, to a degree, gain increased control over behavior.

But, despite Eulau's description, modern political analysis may not be as free from metaphysical discourse as it pretends or desires. Metaphysics and epistemology may not be siblings, but they are intimately related. The analytic principle makes sense only against the backdrop of the cosmology of scientific materialism with its notion of simple location.[87]

There are, however, good reasons, theoretical and practical, to hold the notion of simple location in doubt. On the theoretical level, Whitehead charges the notion of simple location with the "Fallacy of Misplaced Concreteness."[88] The alternative is a cosmology according to which "actuality is through and through togetherness."[89] In Meland's interpretation, this outlook assumes:

> (1) that things exist in relations; (2) that relations are dynamic; (3) that the synthesis of meanings gives rise to a qualitative significance that is not apprehended among isolated events; and (4) that the accumulative effect of attending to such significance is the creation of a qualitative meaning that is over and above pure functional interests.

This is the level of meaning that elicits our profounder emotions, such as appreciation and gratitude, and, under other circumstances, awakens concern and responsible action.[90]

From this perspective, while the analytic process has its contribution to make in the economy of understanding, it is secondary to the act of appreciative consciousness which attends to the communal context and the creative—as well as destructive—potentialities of events.

Furthermore, from this perspective, the act of understanding is itself a mode of practical action. Mind and world are not wholly discrete entities (however much they may appear, as one looks at academic institutions, in a state of divorce). There are, according to Jürgen Habermas, human interests embodied in and through all efforts at knowing, whether those interests are directed toward technical control, cultural understanding, or the emancipation of human action from structures of domination.[91] In any case, the study of public life is always, in some way, an act of public significance.[92]

Habermas would carry the argument one step further, namely, that all efforts at knowing presuppose in principle, even as they may in their actual forms contradict, the paramountcy of interest in full-fledged communicative competence and therefore the overcoming of all forms of alienation.[93] There is, in short, a link, too often neglected, between the search for knowledge and the good life.

Out of a different, but not unsympathetic tradition of thought, John MacMurray suggests that that linkage entails a religious dimension:

The function of religion is the representation of the community of agents, and of the ultimate conditions of action, both in respect of its means and its ends. Religion, we may say, is the knowledge of the Other as community, and is the full form of reflective rationality. It is the knowledge which must inform all action for the achievement of community, and therefore the ground of all really efficient and really satisfactory action whatever.[94]

With a strong note of practical urgency, George Cabot Lodge presses toward the same conclusion:

> Humanity is discovering that, like other species, it is bound by the S-curve that governs growth in any environment. It is clear that the ideology which was effective in governing man's conduct during the first part of the curve, when survival depended upon individual initiative and competition, tooth and claw, must be different from the ideology that will govern the second part of the curve, when survival requires cooperation. . . . The need for social, political, and above all, religious systems by which to recognize and allow for the interrelation of all things—to recognize and give consent to the laws of the whole, whatever we may discover them to be—is the inescapable conclusion of countless modern scientific studies.[95]

Thus Lodge calls for a new structure in the organization of knowledge, a structure in which holism replaces specialization. Holism "is the recognition that everything must be considered in relation to everything else; that mankind is one; that it lives on a spaceship, earth; that the resources available to it are limited; that to survive, men must become harmonious with each other and with all the rest of nature."[96]

From this perspective, there is need for both a critical theory of religion and a critical theory of public life, each of which requires the other for its completion. The ultimate interest of both would be to identify and to overcome structures of alienation wherever they may be found, even in the academy. The ultimate aim of both would effect that kind of emancipation that is directed toward a community of belonging. Perhaps, however, the most that can, at the moment, be expected is the initiation of an elementary community of discourse, a dialogic process cutting across customary disciplinary lines and focused on the meaning and the problem of being a responsible public person within the contemporary world. That in itself, however modest, might epitomize the possibility of reconstructing public life in America. It might recapture a dream that seems almost forgotten.

On that note, I conclude with a statement by Langston Hughes.[97]

O, let America be America again—
The land that never has been yet—
And yet must be—
The land where *every* man is free.
The land that's mine—
The Poor man's, Indian's, Negro's, ME—
Who made America,
Whose sweat and blood, whose faith and pain,
Whose hand at the foundry, whose plow in the rain,
Must bring back our mighty dream again.

O, yes,
I say it plain,
America never was America to me,
And yet I swear this oath—
America will be!
An every-living seed,
Its dream
Lies deep in the heart of me.

We, the people, must redeem
Our land, the mines, the plants, the rivers,
The mountains and the endless plain—

All, all the stretch of these great green states—
And make America again

Notes

1. Robinson Jeffers, "Shine, Perishing Republic," *Robinson Jeffers: Selected Poems* (New York: Vintage Books, 1965), p. 9.

2. Quoted in Sidney Mead, "Religious Pluralism and the Character of the Republic," *Soundings*, 61 (Fall 1978), 313.

3. Roberto M. Unger, *Knowledge and Politics* (New York: The Free Press, 1975), p. 157.

4. Vincent Harding, "Out of the Cauldron of Struggle: Black Religion and the Search for a New America," *Soundings*, 61 (Fall 1978), 339–40.

5. Jürgen Habermas, *Legitimation Crisis* (Boston: Beacon Press, 1975).

6. Robert Heilbroner, *Business Civilization in Decline* (New York: W.W. Norton, 1976).

7. Henry S. Kariel, *Beyond Liberalism: Where Relations Grow* (New York: Harper and Row, 1977).

8. Robert Nisbet, *Twilight of Authority* (New York: Oxford University Press, 1975).

9. Michael Harrington, *The Twilight of Capitalism* (New York: Simon and Schuster, 1976).

10. Albert Eustace Haydon, *The Biography of the Gods* (New York: Macmillan, 1942).

11. Alfred North Whitehead, *Religion in the Making* (New York: Meridian Books, 1960), p. 86.

12. On "principle," see Paul Tillich, *The Socialist Decision* (New York: Harper and Row, 1977), pp. 9–10.

13. Jacques Maritain, *Integral Humanism* (Notre Dame, Ind.: University of Notre Dame Press, 1973).

14. Eduard Heimann, *Reason and Faith in Modern Society: Liberalism, Marxism, and Democracy* (Middletown, Ct.: Wesleyan University Press, 1961).

15. Philip Hefner, "The Foundations of Belonging in a Christian Worldview" in Philip Hefner and Widick Schroeder, eds., *Belonging and Alienation* (Chicago: Center for the Scientific Study of Religion, 1976), pp. 167–68.

16. Whitehead, *Religion in the Making*, p. 86.

17. Bernard Meland, *Higher Education and the Human Spirit* (Chicago: University of Chicago Press, 1953), p. 112.

18. John Dewey, *The Public and Its Problems* (Chicago: The Swallow Press, 1954), chapter 4.

19. *Ibid.*, p. 126.

20. *Ibid.*, p. 134.

21. Hannah Arendt, *Between Past and Future* (New York: Penguin Books, 1978).

22. Robert J. Pranger, *The Eclipse of Citizenship: Power and Participation in Contemporary Politics* (New York: Holt, Rinehart and Winston, 1968).

23. Richard Sennett, *The Fall of Public Man* (New York: Alfred A. Knopf, 1977).

24. Thomas Luckmann, *The Invisible Religion: The Problem of Religion in Modern Society* (New York: Macmillan, 1967).

25. Johann Baptist Metz, *Theology of the World* (New York: Seabury Press, 1969).

26. David Easton, *The Political System: An Inquiry into the State of Political Science* (New York: Alfred A. Knopf, 1953).

27. Thomas Spragens, *The Politics of Motion: The World of Thomas Hobbes* (Lexington, Ky.: University Press of Kentucky, 1973).

28. Unger, *Knowledge and Politics*, p. 63.

29. Frank M. Coleman, *Hobbes and America: Exploring the Constitutional Foundations* (Toronto: University of Toronto Press, 1977).

30. C.B. Macpherson, *The Political Theory of Possessive Individualism: Hobbes to Locke* (London: Oxford University Press, 1962).

31. Coleman, *Hobbes and America*, p. 58.

32. *Leviathan*, I, xiii.

33. William Ernest Hocking, *The Coming World Civilization* (New York: Harper, 1956), p. 30.

34. John MacMurray, *Persons in Relation* (London: Faber and Faber, 1961), p. 17.

35. Bernard Meland, *The Realities of Faith: The Revolution in Cultural Forms* (New York: Oxford University Press, 1962), p. 201.

36. MacMurray, *Persons in Relation*, p. 163.

37. Easton, *The Political System*.

38. *Ibid.*, p. 148.

39. Harold Lasswell, *Politics: Who Gets What, When, How* (Cleveland: Meridian Books, 1958).

40. Kariel, *Beyond Liberalism*, p. 5.

41. *Ibid.*, p. 21.

42. Coleman, *Hobbes and America*, pp. 75–99.

43. *Ibid.*, p. 99.

44. *Ibid.*, pp. 12–23.

45. A.D. Lindsay, *The Modern Democratic State* (London: Oxford University Press, 1943), p. 249.

46. *Ibid.*, pp. 249–68. See also Heimann, *Reason and Faith*, pp. 224–36.

47. Sebastian de Grazia, *Errors of Psychotherapy* (Garden City: Doubleday, 1952), p. 218.

48. Sebastian de Grazia, *The Political Community: A Study of Anomie* (Chicago: The University of Chicago Press, 1948).

49. See Franklin I. Gamwell, "A Discussion of John B. Cobb, Jr., 'The Political Implication of Whitehead's Philosophy'," in John B. Cobb, Jr., and W. Widick Schroeder, eds., *Process Philosophy and Social Thought* (Chicago: Center for the Scientific Study of Religion, 1981), pp. 36–37.

50. Hefner, "The Foundations of Belonging," p. 162.

51. John Smith, *Experience and God* (New York: Oxford University Press, 1968), p. 172.

52. Arendt, *Between Past and Future*, p. 168.

53. *Ibid.*, p. 170.

54. Dewey, *The Public and Its Problems*, pp. 3–36.

55. E.P. Thompson, "Notes on Exterminism, the Last Stage of Civilization," *New Left Review* 121 (May–June, 1980), 3–31.

56. John B. Cobb, Jr., *Is It Too Late? A Theology of Ecology* (Beverly Hills: Bruce, 1972).

57. See, for example, Gayraud Wilmore and James Cone, eds., *Black Theology: A Documentary History* (Maryknoll, N.Y.: Orbis Books, 1979); Rosemary Ruether, *New Woman/New Earth* (New York: Seabury Press, 1975); Letty Russell, *Human Liberation in a Feminist Perspective: A Theology* (Philadelphia: Westminster Press, 1974).

58. Michael Harrington, *Decade of Decision: The Crisis of the American System* (New York: Simon and Schuster, 1980), p. 319.

59. *Ibid.*, p. 320.

60. George Armstrong Kelly, "Mediation Versus Compromise in Hegel," in J. Roland Pennock and John W. Chapman, eds., *Compromise in Ethics, Law and Politics* (New York: New York University Press, 1979), pp. 89–90.

61. *Ibid.*, pp. 91–92.

62. Theodore M. Benditt, "Compromising Interests and Principles," in Pennock and Chapman, eds., *Compromise*, pp. 26–37.

63. Quoted in *ibid.*, p. 28.

64. Martin Golding, "The Nature of Compromise: A Preliminary Inquiry," in Pennock and Chapman, eds., *Compromise*, p. 15.

65. Daniel Maguire, *A New American Justice: Ending White Male Monopolies* (Garden City: Doubleday, 1980).

66. John Rawls, *A Theory of Justice* (Cambridge, Mass.: Harvard University Press, 1971); David A.J. Richards, *The Moral Criticism of Law* (Encino and Belmont, Cal.: Dickenson Publishing Company, 1977).

67. Jacques Maritain, *Man and the State* (Chicago: University of Chicago Press, 1951).

68. Jürgen Moltmann, *The Crucified God* (New York: Harper and Row, 1974).

69. David Miller, *Social Justice* (Oxford: Clarendon Press, 1976); Douglas Sturm, "The Prism of Justice: E Pluribus Unum?" in Thomas Ogletree, ed., *The Annual of the Society of Christian Ethics* (Dallas: Society of Christian Ethics, 1981) pp. 1–28.

70. Robert Nozick, *Anarchy, State and Utopia* (New York: Basic Books, 1974).

71. A.M. Honore, "Social Justice," in Robert S. Summers, ed., *Essays in Legal Philosophy* (Berkeley: University of California Press, 1976), pp. 61–94.

72. Carol Gould, *Marx's Social Ontology: Individuality and Community in Marx's Theory of Social Reality* (Cambridge, Mass.: The M.I.T. Press, 1978).

73. Leo Strauss, *Natural Right in History* (Chicago: University of Chicago Press, 1953).

74. Douglas Sturm, "Constitutionalism: A Critical Appreciation and an Extension of the Political Theory of C.H. McIlwain," *Minnesota Law Review*, 54 (December 1969), 215–44.

75. Douglas Sturm, "Corporations, Constitutions, and Covenants: On Forms of Human Relation and the Problem of Legitimacy," *Journal of the American Academy of Religion*, 41 (September 1973), 331–54.

76. Carl J. Friedrich, *Transcendent Justice: The Religious Dimension of Constitutionalism* (Durham: Duke University Press, 1964).

77. Brian Barry, *Political Argument* (New York: Humanities Press, 1965).

78. Robert Bellah, "Commentary and Proposed Agenda; The Normative Framework for Pluralism in America," *Soundings*, 61 (Fall 1978) 367.

79. Whitehead, *Religion in the Making*, p. 58; see Douglas Sturm, "Prolegomenon to the Reconstruction of the Public Interest," in Franklin Sherman, ed., *American Society of Christian Ethics: Selected Papers* (Chicago: A.S.C.E./Scholars Press, 1975); and "On Meanings of Public Good: An Exploration," *Journal of Religion*, 58 (January 1978), 13–29.

80. Aldo Leopold, *A Sand County Almanac* (New York: Oxford University Press, 1949), p. 214; Cobb, *Is It Too Late?* p. 55.

81. Scott Buchanan, "Natural Law and Teleology," in John Cogley, *et al.*, eds., *Natural Law and Modern Society* (Cleveland: World Publishing Company, 1963), p. 150.

82. Maguire, *A New American Justice*, p. 86.

83. Whitehead, *Religion in the Making*, pp. 58–59.

84. Albert Somit and Joseph Tanenhaus, *The Development of American Political Science: From Burgess to Behaviorism* (Boston: Allyn and Bacon, 1967).

85. Unger, *Knowledge and Politics*, pp. 46–49.

86. Heinz Eulau, *The Behavioral Persuasion in Politics* (New York: Random House, 1963), pp. 9–10. See Douglas Sturm, "Politics and Divinity: Three Approaches in American Political Science," *Thought* 52 (December 1977), 333–65.

87. Alfred North Whitehead, *Science and the Modern World* (New York: Macmillan, 1939).

88. *Ibid.*, pp. 72, 75, 85.

89. *Ibid.*, p. 251.

90. Meland, *Higher Education and the Human Spirit*, p. 24.

91. Jürgen Habermas, *Knowledge and Human Interests* (Boston: Beacon Press, 1971).

92. Coleman, *Hobbes and America*, pp. 153–56.

93. See Fred R. Dallmayr, *Beyond Dogma and Despair: Toward a Critical Phenomenology of Politics* (Notre Dame, Ind.: University of Notre Dame Press, 1981).

94. MacMurray, *Persons in Relation*, p. 185. See also David Tracy, *The Analogical Imagination* (New York: Crossroad, 1981), p. 343.

95. George Cabot Lodge, *The New American Ideology* (New York: Alfred A. Knopf, 1976), p. 226.

96. *Ibid.*, p. 329.

97. Langston Hughes, "Let America Be America Again," in Langston Hughes and Arna Bontemps, eds., *The Poetry of the Negro, 1746–1970* (New York: Anchor Press, 1970), p. 195.

Religion and Reason in American Politics

FRANKLIN I. GAMWELL

WHATEVER HAS BEEN ACHIEVED in the recent debate regarding religion and politics in America, we have not yet clarified the proper place of religion in our public life. All parties endorse the terse formulation of the First Amendment, "Congress shall make no law respecting the establishment of religion, or prohibiting the free exercise thereof,"[1] but there is persisting disagreement about the public philosophy which is there implied. Some fear a secularized state, that is, a state which is independent of all religious convictions, and insist that disestablishment does not preclude a foundation of religious values in the Republic. Others fear a state that is religiously partial and insist that the "wall of separation" prescribes civil neutrality toward religion as such. Each side asserts that the other misrepresents its position. The "religionists," as I will call them, deny that they seek to impose any particular religious conviction; the "separationists," as I will call them, deny that they are hostile to religion.

The problem, as I see it, is that neither party has produced a coherent account, that is, one which makes sense of both its affirmations and its denials. Contemporary religionists typically fail to show how their affirmation of a positive relation between religion and American politics is consistent with their denial of establishment, and contemporary separationists typically fail to show how their affirmation of disestablishment is consistent with their denial of secularism. Each side, then, has good reason to fear what it fears, and the public has good reason to be confused. In this paper, I will try to clarify the grounds of this confusion and the conditions, if any, given which one might be both a religionist and a separationist, that is, might embrace the affirmations of both.

I

This pursuit of clarity should begin with appropriate definitions of religion and politics. Of course, such definitions are themselves subject to extensive controversy. I seek here, therefore, only to stipulate understandings which might command sufficient agreement and provide sufficient precision as to permit a discussion of the relationship between the two activities. The definition of religion must be formal in character, that is, must identify what all religious convictions have in common, because the present problem involves the proper relation between *any* religion and the civil order. Still, this definition must be sufficiently definite so that religion and politics may be distinguished. There is no problem of relationship if the two are identical. The definition of politics should also be formal, at least to the extent that it does not settle arbitrarily the question of how religion properly relates to the civil order.

One of the more well-known proposals with respect to religion is Paul Tillich's claim that a religious commitment is an "ultimate concern,"[2] that is, a concern which informs all of one's life because that to which one is committed is the source of meaning or significance for life itself. Mindful of this proposal, I shall mean by "religion" the affirmation of a comprehensive or all-inclusive purpose or ideal for human life. "Comprehensive" or "all-inclusive" here means a purpose to which all others are properly subservient, an ideal by virtue of which the worth of all possible purposes is properly evaluated. For a religious believer, then, all of his or her activities are properly specifications or parts of his or her religious pursuit. I also intend this definition to include by implication the claim that one's comprehensive purpose is authentic, in the sense that it is not merely a private or subjective choice or preference but is the all-inclusive ideal which humans as such ought to pursue. Still, the definition is formal in character. It neither identifies some particular comprehensive purpose which it asserts to be authentic nor even asserts that human existence can be said to have one. Thus, I mean only to stipulate that all religious convictions have in common the *claim* that humans are bound to some such ideal.

A clear illustration of religious purpose is the double commandment found in the New Testament Gospel of Matthew: "You shall love the Lord your God with all your heart, and with all your soul, and with all your mind. . . . You shall love your neighbor as yourself." But this is an example, not an alternative formulation, of the definition offered. Religion as formally defined does not necessarily include belief in God, as some Eastern religions confirm, nor even an explicit claim about "ultimate reality." More often than not, perhaps, religions do assert something about the fundamental nature of things. In order to secure the broadest possible definition that remains serviceable, however, I seek to include those all-inclusive claims which are "merely ethical," that is, which assert a comprehensive purpose that is thought to be independent of any metaphysical convictions. It has been said of John Dewey, for instance, that "his guiding intention throughout an extraordinarily long and influential career may be summarized as the attempt to further the realization of democracy in every sphere of life,"[3] and, indeed, Dewey himself explicitly argued for a merely ethical religion.[4]

What is distinctive about religion, then, is the comprehensive character of the purpose in question, and it is this character which permits a difference between religion and politics. I will define "politics" formally as the activities of the state and the process by which those activities are decided or determined. The "state," in turn, refers to that association whose identifying purpose is to order or govern the pursuit of purposes in the community and is, therefore, the one association in any society to which all individuals in the society must belong. Accordingly, the civil order is granted for its purpose the legitimate use of coercion. It then follows that the purpose of the state is not necessarily comprehensive. To begin with, the governance of a state generally concerns the purposes within a given society, in distinction from all human purposes. In addition, as the United States Constitution illustrates, the civil order may be understood properly to coerce human purposes only in certain limited respects, thereby leaving a range of human activity and association voluntary. Perhaps, in contrast, totalitarian governments have at least approached the claim that the state's purpose is, within the society in question, all-inclusive, and, conceivably, a state with pretensions to rule the entire world might make a claim that is comprehensive. But such a claim could only assert an identity between certain substantive understandings of religion and politics, and it remains that the two are formally distinct. Formally speaking, religion is comprehensive by definition while politics is not, so that these definitions permit a question regarding the proper relationship between the two in the American Republic.

Clearly, those who advocate a foundation of religious values in the Republic do not assert that the state's purpose is a religious one. But it does not follow, religionists maintain, that politics cannot or should not be based upon a religious ideal, in the sense that the limited purposes of the state are properly informed or guided by a comprehensive purpose. Just which aspects of life in the community are subject to regulation by the civil order might be properly decided in accord with some understanding of the comprehensive ideal for human life. For religious believers, moreover, this must be the case. To affirm a comprehensive ideal is to assert that this purpose is the inclusive context in which all human activities, including political ones, should be evaluated, so that non-comprehensive or limited purposes are properly specifications of the inclusive ideal to the particular circumstances in question. Those who hold that all human life should be lived in love of God and neighbor necessarily believe that the activities of the state should conform to that ideal. Associational life should be subject to coercion precisely insofar as this is required to promote or to maximize the love that is comprehensively commanded. Similarly, Dewey's commitment to the realization of democracy in all spheres of life provides for those who agree the proper context in which to evaluate proposed public purposes.

When the "wall of separation" is said to mean civil neutrality toward religion as such, contemporary religionists often take this to assert that the public purpose should not be informed by a religious ideal, and, given the formal definition of religious ideals as comprehensive, this assertion would imply the secularistic claim that no religious convictions are true. Thus, the issue for these religious believers is whether one can be with integrity both a person of religious faith and an American citizen, where the latter includes adherence to the First Amendment. If the state cannot be informed by religious purposes, they argue, then either their faith is mocked or their citizenship revoked. Thus, they continue, this understanding of the civil order renders the freedom of religion meaningless, since the latter protects only those religions which do not advance comprehensive ideals, that is, which are not religions at all. Some separationists only seem to confirm this reading when they say that religion in America is a strictly private affair, that is, a belief to be confessed intimately but irrelevant to the political process. In any event, it is not clear how separationists propose to be otherwise understood. They have not shown, to the best of my knowledge, how their insistence upon disestablishment avoids by implication the denial of religion altogether.

But if the issue for religionists is whether one *can* be a religiously committed American citizen, the issue for separationists is whether one *must* be religiously committed in order to be a citizen. Unless the state is neutral to religion as such, this argument runs, religious commitment is prescribed as a condition of citizenship. Separationists may point out that this condition would be inconsistent with the constitutional prohibition of a religious test for public office. Since public officials must be citizens, a religious test for citizenship is implicitly proscribed. Moreover, some may argue, only neutrality in this sense prevents the establishment of a particular religious conviction. There is, after all, no such thing as religion in general; we have only the several and distinct religions (Christianity, Judaism, Islam, etc.), each of which affirms its own understanding of life's comprehensive ideal. The state's activities cannot be informed by two or more differing religious purposes because, at some point, differing comprehensive ideals will prescribe inconsistent political policies. Nor can one consistently hold that political purposes should at one time be guided by one certain religious ideal and at some other time by another. Were this the case, one would need, per impossible, an even more comprehensive purpose by virtue of which properly to decide which religious ideal is appropriate on which occasions. In sum, religious foundations for the Republic must be the same for all state activities, that is, some particular religion must be constitutive of the civil order. But this, the argument concludes, is the witting or unwitting endorsement of an established religion.

The apparent logic of this position only seems confirmed when some who advocate a positive relation between religion and politics seem to have a particular religion in mind, usually a version of Christianity or, if there is such a thing, of the "Judaeo-Christian" tradition. Nor is the charge answered when others, seeking to appropriate a classic essay by Robert Bellah,[5] affirm a general "civil religion," which purportedly is distinct from all of the commonly recognized religious traditions but constitutive of American political ideals.[6] If this civil religion provides grounds for evaluating the state's activities, separationists will argue, then it must include some identifiable understanding of life's comprehensive purpose, and its adherents thus seem to advocate establishment. In any event, it is not clear how religionists propose to avoid this consequence. To the best of my knowledge, they have not shown how their insistence upon religious foundations for the Republic avoids by implication a denial of disestablishment.

If this general summary of the recent discussion is more or less adequate, the issue may seem irresolvable. Each party seeks to protect something important. Religionists seek to insure the legitimacy of religious commitment; separationists guard disestablishment. But neither has answered the telling criticism of the other. Neither party, then, seems coherently to affirm the disestablishment of religion—religionists because they seemingly deny establishment, separationists because they seemingly deny religion. But the First Amendment is the one thing in this whole matter which everyone claims to affirm. The public does have reason to be confused.[7]

II

Should we conclude from this confusion that the dispute reveals an impasse, one disquieting consequence would be a severe judgment against those architects of the Republic who were principally responsible for the understanding of religion and politics prescribed in the First Amendment. For we will have decided that the disestablishment of religion is a contradiction in terms, that is, neither of the principal terms can be affirmed without denying the other. Given the esteem in which Americans generally hold the political wisdom of Thomas Jefferson, Benjamin Franklin and James Madison, to name three of the more prominent, this consequence may suggest that something is still amiss. In the remainder of this paper, I wish to argue that a reasonable understanding of the First Amendment is available within—or, at least, through—the thought of those who designed it. My purpose here is principally constructive rather than historical, that is, I am concerned to recommend an understanding of religion in American political life rather than to show precisely what understandings were present in the minds of the significant founders of the Republic. Accordingly, I will seek only to summarize the theory of the founders and, moreover, to present that theory in its most coherent form.

In turning to the thought of the founders, I do not mean to assert that the disestablishment of religion in America was principally the result of a particular philosophy. The American experiment with religious freedom constituted a major break with the relation between religion and politics traditionally practiced in European civilization, and major changes in political or religious history are rarely the effect of thought alone. In the present case, as many students of American history have argued, the accidents of history had created in the American colonies such a measure of religious diversity that religious freedom in some form was probably unavoidable if these colonies were to be united. Congregationalists and Baptists peopled New England; Anglicans dominated Virginia and most of the south; Presbyterians, Quakers, Lutherans, Roman Catholics and others were numerous in the middle territories. No one of these churches was strong enough to make good on a bid to be the official religion of the new nation. Any such attempt would have been successfully resisted by a coalition of the others, and the nation would have been stillborn were establishment in the usual sense a prerequisite.

It is true that all of the numerically significant religious communities were Christian, and it might be argued that the establishment of Christianity as such was a possibility. This would not have allowed an official church in the sense which includes some unified institutional expression, but a Christian test for public office might have been stipulated and all citizens might have been required in some specified way to support the activities of some Christian church or other. But if such "multiple establishment" was a possibility, then the rejection of this alternative in favor of full disestablishment only underscores what I wish to argue: whatever part the sheer fact of religious diversity may have played in the American religious experiment, it was the thought of the founders which made most sense of it. Major changes in political and religious institutions also rarely occur simply by virtue of the accidents of history. They must be given formulation in the human mind and reason in relation to human ideals, and it was this that the thought of the founders introduced.

As it happens, bringing reason into political life was a principal purpose of the founders, or at least of those who were most significant with respect to the disestablishment of religion. Because they were children of the European Age of Enlightenment, often otherwise called the Age of Reason, they were typically convinced that individual life fulfills its potential and the body politic is perfected insofar as each is guided by rational reflection. With respect to the political process, this implied that opportunities for full rational discussion and debate should be secured. The errors or prejudices of irrational claims could be disclosed by the light of criticism and the truth could be approached by the common reflection of inherently fallible individuals. Precisely because religion involves the comprehensive purpose by virtue of which all others are evaluated, the commitment to reason required the disestablishment of religion. Were some particular religious conviction endorsed by the coercive powers of the state, full debate regarding the public purpose would be compromised. "Religious freedom was clearly envisaged as the deliberate creation of a situation where every religious opinion and practice, having the right to free expression, would continually contend with all others in order that error might be exposed to view and the truth be recognized."[8]

Does this reliance upon reasonable public discussion mean that Jefferson, Franklin, and the rest sought to secularize the civil order? On the contrary, all of the significant founders affirmed the existence of God and, consistently, believed that the Republic would fail in its commission unless its purposes were responsive to the transcendent or divine will. Their speeches and writings are replete with references to the relation between the new nation and the purposes of God. As Enlightenment thinkers, however, and this is the crucial point, they were also convinced that religion is a rational matter, in the sense that the nature of ultimate reality and the substantive character of life's comprehensive ideal are accessible to or understandable through common human experience and reason. " 'Reason' . . . did not mean merely the process of reasoning, but a basic principle of human nature through which man, the creature, was enabled to read the great revelation of the Creator in His works and shape his conduct accordingly."[9]

Each of these men had his own more or less clear and consistent view of religious truth, even if, when we read their formulations, the substance of these views seems relatively thin.
So Franklin, for one, wrote in his autobiography: "I never
doubted the existence of Deity; that he made the world and
governed it by his providence; that the most acceptable service
to God was the doing of good to men; that our souls are immortal; and that all crime will be punished, and virtue rewarded, either here or hereafter."[10] But the substance of such
formulations is not the important consideration here. The
point of moment is that authentic religious beliefs, whatever
their substance in fact is, are inherently accessible to humans
qua humans, or inherently rational in character. Given this
conviction, the genuine disestablishment of religion was coherent with a positive relation between religion and politics,
because the state's purposes could be evaluated or informed by
the religious truth that would be distilled in a full public debate. Just insofar as public discussion was successful, in other
words, public policy would be based upon the authentic religious ideal.

Some may object that this solution does not really avoid
an established religion. If the state's activities are informed by
a religious debate, then is it not the case that those religious
convictions which are most persuasive to the public and which,
therefore, guide public policy become ipso facto established?
Let us suppose, to clarify the objection with a contemporary
example, that debate among the religions makes increasingly
persuasive the claim that abortion is (with, perhaps, severely
limited exceptions) contrary to the will of God, and, consequently, the state proscribes abortion. Why should we not say
that a particular religious conviction has been established in the
nation's laws? Something very like this argument was advanced by the plaintiffs in *McRae v. Califano*. Opposing the so-
called Hyde Amendment of 1976, which banned the use of

federal funds for abortions and which had been vigorously supported on religious grounds, the plaintiffs argued that this law in effect established a religious view of the beginnings of human life.

But this line of thought misunderstands the meaning of religious establishment as it could only have been intended by the founders. By previous European practice, established religion meant a church which was explicitly declared to be official for the nation, such that citizens were in some way required to support the explicit teaching of its beliefs. That the laws of the state might be implicitly religious, because they are informed by some understanding of life's comprehensive purpose, is quite another matter. Precisely because they were themselves religious believers, the founders could not consistently have sought to prevent the implicitly religious character of the state's activities, and their own insistence upon the Republic's obligation to the divine purpose confirms the point. Given that one affirms some religious claim, it follows, as we have seen, that every human purpose, including those of politics, should be implicitly guided by it, and it was just this that the founders sought to insure through the provision for full and reasonable debate. Contrary to the plaintiffs in *McRae*, then, there is no violation of the First Amendment in the federal proscription of abortion, even assuming that this law is implicitly committed to some particular religious conviction. For such a law prescribes no explicit teaching of religion.[11]

With contemporary religionists, then, the founders' understanding of the First Amendment affirms the importance of authentic religion to the Republic. With contemporary separationists, it also affirms a separation between the churches and the state. The two affirmations are consistently advanced by virtue of a distinction between the *explicit* activities of the state, which should never include support for the teaching of religion, and the *implicit* religious ideal by which the laws are properly informed. Moreover, the distinction between explicit state activity and its implicit religious foundations can be meaningfully affirmed because religious claims are held to be rational, so that the influence of religion upon public policy can be assigned to the process of public debate. If we wish to use the term "civil religion" to mean those religious convictions which are implied by a particular political policy or set of policies, then we may say that the civil religion, far from being constitutive of the Republic in the sense that all citizens are bound to it, is precisely what the founders left to public debate.

It follows that the state's explicit activities are non-comprehensive in character. At the least, the explicit teaching of religion and, therefore, the substantial religious claims advocated and criticized in public discussion cannot be legitimately coerced but remain entirely dependent upon the voluntariness of individuals and associations.[12] It also follows that the religious debate can never be terminated nor its results ever given official formulation. The only respect in which this debate reaches a conclusion is the provisional and implicit expression it receives in the non-comprehensive decisions about public policy. Of course, the state requires some appropriate process through which the public discussion informs political decisions. Although I will not pursue the matter here, to ask about that process is, at least in the American Republic, to ask about the proper forms of democratic decision.

In appropriating this understanding of the First Amendment, one need not suggest that public discussion of any given issue should begin with or even include explicit discussion of alternative religious convictions. On the contrary, political debates most often arise in terms of particular proposed policies or changes in policy and sometimes properly run their course without self-conscious attention to the most fundamental grounds for evaluation. This latter will be the case when the public disagreement concerns the facts relevant to the issue in question, including divergent estimates of the probable consequences of a given policy, while the relevant values to be affirmed are non-controversial at a relatively low level of generality. According to the founders' understanding, however, there is properly present in such cases the tacit assumption that values commonly affirmed are consistent with the comprehensive purpose which would be most persuasive were debate to occur at that level, so that the policy which is eventually enacted implies authentic religion.

III

Assuming that the founders' thought made sense of the religious experiment in eighteenth century America, we must ask nonetheless whether it makes sense of religious disestablishment in our present context. In this regard, the most important aspect of the theory we have reviewed is the founders' more or less unquestioned conviction that some religious claims are indeed authentic. "I never doubted the existence of the Deity," wrote Franklin, and, as I have mentioned, other principal founders refer repeatedly to the constitutive importance of religion or the divine purpose for the life of the Republic. For some readers, these references provide evidence that an identifiable or substantive religion was for these men properly constitutive of the new nation. As I have suggested, however, this reading would introduce inconsistency into the original understanding of the First Amendment. If a particular religious conviction or set of convictions is said to be constitutive of the body politic, then it would be inconsistent to proscribe explicit teaching of that religion by the state. Such teaching would be nothing other than teaching the meaning of the constitution itself, that is, the meaning of good citizenship. Accordingly, I suggest that the founders' theory is most coherent if these references are read as expressions of a formal understanding of religion, in the sense which I defined earlier. To be sure, they apparently took the existence of God for granted, but this simply betrays, I will assume, the fact that eighteenth century Americans could not imagine a non-theistic religion. By this reading, then, the references to religion do not properly intend a particular or substantive conception of life's comprehensive ideal. Instead they assert only that the Republic should be informed by authentic religion, whatever it is, so that the content or substance of that religious foundation is the subject for public debate among candidate formulations. With respect to religion, the only explicit teaching permitted to the state would be adherence to the conditions of reasonable debate.

Still, the fact that the founders "never doubted" may, in our context, raise doubt about their theory. If the interpretation which I have presented keeps the state explicitly independent of any particular or substantive religious claim, it nonetheless leaves public policy dependent upon some religious convictions, however implicit they may be and however open to debate is their material content. But significant numbers of twentieth century Americans do not consider themselves religious at all. In response, it might be noted that the formal definition of religion which has informed this discussion is unusually broad, since it stipulates that religion is present wherever there is a conviction regarding the comprehensive purpose of human life. Thus, religion does not necessarily include a theistic belief nor, for that matter, any explicit affirmations regarding the ultimate nature of reality, and such metaphysical affirmations are often what people intend to deny when they claim to be non-religious. Since citizens who so claim must nonetheless advance some fundamental grounds for the evaluation of public policy, it might be argued that these grounds, by virtue of being fundamental, constitute a comprehensive purpose or ideal for human life. Given the broad definition of religion, in other words, it might be said that all citizens are inescapably religious.

But this issue turns upon how the term "comprehensive" is here understood. If it is taken to mean simply the fundamental grounds for moral evaluation, then religion has indeed been defined with sufficient breadth to include citizens as such.[13] However, some may object that the problem of relating religion and American politics has now been solved only by so changing the meaning of "religious" that it applies to citizens who would be offended to be so described. For this reason, I earlier offered a more strict definition of "comprehensive purpose," namely, a purpose to which all others are subservient, such that all human activities should be a part of the religious pursuit. In contrast to this use of "comprehensive," one may in fact assert fundamental grounds for political evaluation that are non-religious. Some have claimed, for instance, that the body politic should insure the equal freedom of all its citizens, where this means equal opportunity to live life by their own lights or to pursue their own chosen interests. Indeed, it might be said that this understanding is especially widespread in contemporary America. In any event, equal freedom or equal opportunity here constitutes the fundamental grounds for political evaluation, even though it is not the case that all of one's activities are properly embraced by the pursuit of these values. On the contrary, these values are simply conditions for each citizen to seek his or her particular interests.

But once we agree that religion should not be so understood as to make all citizens religious by definition, then separationists might object to the theory of the founders. By assuming that some religious claims are authentic, this objection runs, the founders made citizenship inherently religious, and thereby secured a positive relation between religion and politics only by disenfranchising those who refuse all religious claims. However inconsequential that price may have been in the eighteenth century, the objection continues, the disestablishment of religion in our time properly means civil neutrality toward religion as such, including the choice between affirming some or denying all religious convictions. It may then seem to religionists that religious foundations for the Republic have again been denied, so that, the founders notwithstanding, we return to a contemporary impasse.[14]

But this conclusion is premature. Civil neutrality toward religion as such need not be a denial of religious truth, and the possibility of this resolution is, I hold, introduced by the reading of the founders that I have presented. We may, in other words, reformulate the founders' theory so as clearly to leave in question what they took for granted. What permits this reformulation is precisely their overriding conviction that the authenticity of religious claims may be tested by humans qua human. However much they "never doubted," they nonetheless believed that *whether* life is subject to a comprehensive ideal, as well as *what* that ideal is, is a question the answer to which is accessible to common experience and reason.

I propose, therefore, that we now understand the relation between religion and politics in America—and, therefore, the First Amendment—in the following way. The state's defining purpose is to govern life within the society, which purpose is understood to be non-comprehensive, such that some human decisions are not properly subject to governmental coercion. Specifically, the state is constitutionally proscribed from teaching whether or not human life is subject to a comprehensive purpose. It then follows that the state also may not teach a particular understanding of life's comprehensive purpose, since this activity would simultaneously teach that life does have such a purpose, or teach a particular understanding of non-religious but fundamental grounds for moral evaluation, since this activity would simultaneously teach that there is no authentic religion. The civil order must remain explicitly neutral to claims for and against religion as such and, therefore, claims regarding the fundamental grounds for moral evaluation. The truth of these claims properly belongs to the public debate, and the debate is now understood to include not only advocates of differing religions but also those who are persuaded that all religious claims are false. Whether or not life has a comprehensive purpose may be called the comprehensive question; it may also be called the religious question, even if the answer to which one adheres denies all religious claims. Thus, we may say that religious disestablishment prohibits the state from explicitly giving an answer to the religious question. Public purposes, then, should be implicitly informed by that answer to the comprehensive or religious question and, therefore, by the fundamental grounds for evaluation which the process of public debate reveals to be most convincing.

It follows that neither the affirmation nor the denial of religious truth is a condition of American citizenship. On the contrary, the only required commitment is to laws which are informed by the truth that is accessible to common experience and reason. Citizens qua citizens properly assert the following: If the truth about human life is its obligation to some comprehensive ideal, then this ideal, whatever it is, should be implicit in the laws of the state; if the truth about human life excludes all religious claims, then the activities of the state should be informed by whatever rational grounds remain in view of which public policies might be evaluated. This is, of course, nothing other than a commitment to rational debate with respect to public purposes and, given common consent to this, all else is subject to public review.

With this interpretation, religionists have no reason to claim that disestablishment denies religious truth. Whether any religious claims are true has been left to debate, and those who hold to the affirmative are urged publicly to present their reasons. Insofar as any given religion is true, and insofar as the public debate is successful, then precisely that religion will guide the activities of the state. Nor can separationists claim that this interpretation requires citizens to be religious. If no religion is true, and insofar as the public debate is successful, the state's activities will be secularistic in character. Because the answer to the comprehensive question is not the explicit business of the state, the Republic as such is neither dependent upon nor independent of religious convictions.

Separationists, then, are wrong if they proclaim that religious claims do not belong within American politics. To seek the political implications of one's faith, and to advocate both in the public debate, is not only permitted to but incumbent upon citizens of the Republic, since the import of disestablishment is to insure the fullness of that rational debate upon which the well-being of the Republic depends. Thus, we should disagree with those who assert that religiously committed citizens violate the American political process by introducing religious convictions into the public debate about abortion, nuclear deterrence, or the appropriate character of the economy. But this defense of religiously committed political participation can be sustained only if we simultaneously underscore the one condition of citizenship which the First Amendment includes—namely, the commitment to rational debate. Those who would advocate religious grounds for public policy are required to defend their convictions by appeal to considerations that can be assessed by all members of the public. Further, they should be prepared to entertain reasoned criticism of their commitments and, therefore, be open to the possibility that rational reflection will show these commitments to be in greater or lesser measure false. Absent the willingness to be persuaded as well as to persuade, one is not a genuine participant in reasonable debate. Moreover, separationists may with justice claim, religionists in America have all too often failed to honor this condition of their citizenship. It is common for religiously committed Americans to advocate positions on abortion, national defense, the economy and other public issues on the basis of religious convictions which they are not prepared to test and defend in public debate. As a consequence, those who disagree cannot be engaged in discussion but only dismissed, and the logic of that course leads only to religious belligerence and civil instability.

At this point, some religious believers will object that the nature of their faith does not permit the simultaneous concession that their convictions may be false. Indeed, it is widely thought today, in contrast to the view of the founders, that religious convictions are inherently non-rational or "beyond reason," so that every religious belief is "simply a matter of faith" in the sense that a particular faith commitment cannot be reasonably questioned or assessed. In my judgment, however, whatever force this objection seems to have derives solely from the fact that it is widely assumed to be true. Notwithstanding its prevalent appeal, in other words, I see no persuasive case for this understanding of religion. On the contrary, there is always a basic distinction between the fact that one believes something and the fact, if it is one, that one's belief is valid or credible, and reasoning assessment is the way in which we test for credibility. In other words, the sheer acknowledgement that humans are fallible, in the sense that any belief may be mistaken, is a reservation which appropriately accompanies any other conviction, including a religious one. This recognition does not compromise the fact that one genuinely believes what one believes, or even that one is firmly convinced. It is, rather, a part of the meaning of human belief itself, so that the firmest conviction is not only consistent with but implies the reservation that further evidence and argument may change one's mind. In short, the requirement that religious advocacy regarding public issues participate in a reasonable debate is itself a thoroughly reasonable condition.

The widely held assumption that religious convictions are immune to the light of public examination is, I submit, the most fundamental cause of contemporary confusion about religion and politics in America. For its acceptance permits only establishment or secularism. Absent the requirement that one's religious beliefs must be credible in terms of common experience and reason, one has no grounds upon which to affirm a full public discussion as the process by which public policy is decided. On the contrary, the public cannot be persuaded to affirm supposed truths which are not accessible to humans qua humans, so that one's comprehensive ideal can purposefully inform the Republic only if there is a religious test for public office and/or if the state supports the teaching of this religious conviction. It then follows that one denies establishment only as a witting or unwitting secularist, for one thereby denies any positive relation between religion and the civil order. The generally unexamined claim that religious convictions do not admit of public debate is shared by most contemporary religionists and separationists alike, so that the former typically deny disestablishment while they affirm religion and the latter typically deny religion while they affirm disestablishment. The view that religious truth is accessible to reason is, then, a necessary condition for affirming in a coherent manner both the possibility of authentic religion and its disestablishment.[15] Accordingly, it should be said clearly that convictions which will not submit to rational review have no claim upon the attention of the American public nor, therefore, upon the regard of individuals qua citizens. For the First Amendment prescribes allegiance to rational debate.

For the founders of our country, the commitment to rational debate was nothing other than the indispensable character of citizenship insofar as the body politic is to be perfected. It was their legacy from the Enlightenment to believe that human life, both private and public, is fulfilled insofar as it is informed by rational reflection. Thus, another name for allegiance to the First Amendment is simply the commitment to civility—and, in turn, civility means not a passive tolerance because little really matters but an active engagement in public affairs before the bar of reason. It then follows that citizenship cannot be properly understood as simply an extension of one's pursuit of self-interest. To the contrary, civility requires the willingness to sacrifice self-interest in order to participate in the reasonable pursuit of public good. As a consequence, it may also be called civic virtue.

Because the commitment to public argument properly extends to the most comprehensive or religious question, we may underscore the fundamental character of civic virtue by calling it religious civility. Against some contemporary secularists, I commend for the public's considered response all religiously committed political advocacy which repudiates establishment because it seeks to engage in reasoned debate. I also urge the public to ignore religious incivility wherever it appears.

Notes

1. In this essay, I will not discuss the difference and possible conflict between the two religion clauses in the First Amendment. As will become apparent, I am concerned with the proper place, if any, of religion in the political process, such that the constitutional prohibition of establishment is here the relevant clause. The protection of religious freedom, then, is here discussed only insofar as it is an implication of disestablishment.

2. See Paul Tillich, *Dynamics of Faith* (New York: Harper and Row, 1957).

3. Robert Horowitz, "John Dewey," in *History of Political Philosophy*, ed. by Leo Strauss and Joseph Cropsey (Chicago: Rand McNally and Company, 1963), p. 746.

4. John Dewey, *A Common Faith* (New Haven: Yale University Press, 1934).

5. Robert N. Bellah, "Civil Religion in America," *Daedalus*, 96 (Winter, 1967).

6. See Charles Krauthammer, "America's Holy War," *The New Republic*, April 9, 1984.

7. My understanding of the founders' thought regarding the disestablishment of religion is indebted to the work of Sidney E. Mead. See Sidney E. Mead, *The Lively Experiment: The Shaping of Christianity in America* (New York: Harper and Row, 1963) and *The Nation with the Soul of a Church* (New York: Harper and Row, 1975).

8. Mead, *The Lively Experiment*, p. 82.

9. *Ibid.*, p. 61.

10. Cited in *ibid.*, p. 64.

11. My argument here is designed only to illustrate—and, therefore, is based solely upon—the understanding of the disestablishment clause which I have presented. I do not intend to judge whether the plaintiffs in *McRae* persuasively argued their First Amendment claim in relation to the tests for establishment previously formulated by the Supreme Court. Should the judgment in that regard be affirmative, however, I would then wish to ask about the coherence of the theory implied in the Court's formulations. For the sake of clarity, I should also note that nothing I have said intends to present an argument for or against the prohibition of abortion.

12. In saying this, I do not deny that the United States Constitution generally, and the First Amendment particularly, also specify many other respects in which purposes may not be legitimately coerced. My point is simply that the disestablishment clause alone entails the noncomprehensive character of the state's activities.

13. Based upon just such a definition of religion, I myself claimed in an earlier essay that the First Amendment requires Amer-

ican citizens to be religious. See Franklin I. Gamwell, "Religion and the Public Purpose," *Journal of Religion*, 62 (1982), pp. 284–85. As the present text goes on to suggest, however, I now think that religion should be more precisely—and, therefore, more strictly—defined. Still, the substantive point that I wish to make, namely, that the First Amendment prohibits the state from teaching any view of the fundamental grounds for evaluation, may be formulated given either definition.

14. My understanding of the relation between religious claims and common experience and reason is indebted to Schubert M. Ogden. To the best of my knowledge, Ogden is the Christian theologian who has formulated this matter most clearly and systematically. See Schubert M. Ogden, "The Task of Philosophical Theology," in *The Future of Philosophical Theology*, ed. by Robert A. Evans (Philadelphia: Westminster Press, 1971), pp. 55–84; "What Is Theology?" *Journal of Religion*, 52 (1972), pp. 22–40; and *Faith and Freedom: Toward a Theology of Liberation* (Nashville: Abingdon, 1979), esp. pp. 115–24.

15. Contrary to the argument presented above, some may claim that a religious believer might coherently affirm both a non-rational religious conviction and disestablishment if his or her religion prescribes tolerance of other faiths. Something like this is at least one reading of the grounds upon which John Courney Murray recommended the First Amendment to American Roman Catholics. See John Courtney Murray, *We Hold These Truths: Catholic Reflections on the American Proposition* (New York: Sheed and Ward, Inc., 1960). But this resolution does not avoid an implied commitment to religious establishment. If the prescription of religious tolerance is indeed dependent upon the non-rational tenets of one's particular religion (if, that is, the latter is a necessary condition of the former), then the First Amendment could not be coherently affirmed unless this particular religion is also affirmed. In that event, the First Amendment would (inconsistently) prescribe that citizens be taught to adhere to the religion in question. If, to the contrary, it is said that these particular religious convictions are not a necessary condition for religious tolerance, then the religious convictions do not constitute a comprehensive purpose, i.e., do not constitute a religion in the sense that I have

been using the term. Religious tolerance is now publicly prescribed on secularistic grounds. In sum, adherence to disestablishment must be possible without adherence to any particular religious convictions. Given that a religion affirms some comprehensive purpose, I hold that the First Amendment can mean nothing other than the recognition of human fallibility and the commitment to public assessment of religious claims.

PART TWO

EXPLORATIONS

Particular Classics, Public Religion, and the American Tradition

DAVID TRACY

I

MY AIM IN THIS BRIEF PAPER is to explore a question: Do particular traditions bear public resources? The answer is not obvious. But the refusal to pose the question, I suggest, has hampered many discussions of the role of religion in public life.

Consider the contemporary discussion of the nature of publicness itself. In a pluralist culture, it is important to know what will and will not count as public—i.e., available to all intelligent, reasonable and responsible members of that culture despite their otherwise crucial differences in belief and practice. A public realm assumes that there is the possibility of discussion (argument, conversation) among various participants. The only hope for such discussion in a radically pluralist culture is one based on reason. Yet to state that reason is needed is to restate the problem of publicness, not to resolve it.

For what can it mean to say that all parties in a pluralist culture (individuals, groups, traditions) can meet in the public realm, the realm of reason, if there does not seem to be a shared (public) understanding of reason itself?[1] If reason can only function instrumentally, for example, then the culture can reasonably agree on the appropriate instrumental (especially technological) means to achieve its ends, but the ends—the shared values—are, by definition, private, decisionistic, non-rational. And this problem—the so-called problem of instrumental reason and resultant technicization of the once public realm—is intensified by the contemporary insistence (in philosophy, ethics and theology alike) that reason itself has a history. To affirm the latter is to pose yet another problem for publicness: the problem that various models of reason are themselves *in some sense* dependent on particular social, cultural, historical forces. Has publicness itself now been rendered private?

The fact that the problem of the historicity of reason has surfaced most tellingly in reflections upon the truth-claims of the "hard sciences" themselves (or, more exactly, among philosophers of science such as Kuhn, Toulmin, and Putnam)[2] has only made the problem of the public realm that much more difficult. For the rule of a purely "instrumental reason"—and thereby the technicization of a once public realm—can only be further empowered if the "checks and balances" on technical reason via the methods of verification and falsification in the "hard sciences" are themselves now interpreted as in some crucial sense historically bound. Indeed radical proposals to this effect can readily be found in Feyerabend and Rorty even before deconstructionist literary theorists have had their say on the social sciences and the humanities.[3]

This much seems clear in the present debate over the character of reason (and, therefore, the nature of publicness itself): earlier debates with strictly positivist understandings of natural science (and, by extension, of reason) and strictly instrumentalist understandings of the relationships of techniques and values (and, by extension, the technicization of the public realm) are now spent. The major discussion (and a far more difficult one) has shifted elsewhere: Does the collapse of the over-claims of positivism and instrumentalism mean that what little remained left in the public realm (viz., positivist and instrumentalist notions of reason) is now itself gone. Must we, therefore, resign ourselves to the absence of *any* public realm at all and the destruction of any "hard" notion of "publicness"?

I paint this picture, at once bleak and too brief, of the contemporary discussion of reason or publicness not to induce the claims of Feyerabend or Rorty or Derrida. I paint it, rather, to suggest that the question of religion in the public realm is a question that can clarify both the character of the truth-claims of religion and the character of any claim to truth in the public realm itself. For the fact is, as Richard Bernstein's article elsewhere in this volume shows, there remain many thinkers who defend the public realm and rationality itself.[4] These thinkers (Toulmin, Putnam, and Kuhn himself could be added to Bernstein's list) defend the possibilities of "publicness" and "reason" without retreating into either a-historical positivist or instrumentalist notions of "reason." They also defend rationality without endorsing positions so radically pluralistic that they are finally indistinguishable from classic forms of hard relativism or historicism, however bedecked in the more attractive apparel of the "radical indeterminacy of meaning" and the always elusive, if not illusory, character of "truth" itself.

If the problems of publicness and rationality (and thereby of the public realm) are as difficult as Bernstein in his several works and his present article shows and as I suggest above, then the introduction of "religion" into this debate may seem singularly unpromising. What seems more obviously "private" than religion? Religion seems private not just in the sociological sense of privatization but private in the philosophical sense of "without reason," decisionistic, undemonstrated, and perhaps undemonstrable. There are, in fact, ethical and theological analogues to the kinds of options represented in philosophy of science by Feyerabend or Rorty. Through the discovery of the historical roots and narrative forms of reason itself, such ethicists as Alasdair MacIntyre can seem to leave us with but two choices: Nietzsche or a new St. Benedict.[5] The choices are, indeed, both apt and disheartening for the public realm: the deconstructionist recovery of the "new Nietzsche" is, thus far, hardly conducive to revitalizing the public realm of ethics and politics.[6] And many of the new Christian "narrative theologies" are self-consciously sectarian.

In this discussion, one crucial need is to shift the major focus of the debate away from "origins" to "effects." More exactly, one can agree with (indeed learn thankfully from) the present rediscoveries of the historical and communal (narrative) roots or origins of all models of publicness and reason. And yet we should remain utterly unpersuaded by their conclusions on effects—viz., that all we have are particular traditions (of both reason and religion) whose particularist effects are as non-public, non-shareable as their origins. In Troeltschian terms this translates into the position that there is no church; there are only sects. In ethical terms, this translates into the insistence that no Kant-like enterprise ever has or could succeed; only various aretaic positions grounded in particular communities and narratives are possible. In more general philosophical terms, this translates as: there are no persuasive transcendental or metaphysical arguments; there is only context-bound rhetorical persuasion within concrete communities of discourse. In general theological terms, this translates: there is no fundamental theology; there are only various systematic theologies. In terms of our present set of questions, this translates: there is no authentic public realm where a public, shared reason can rule; there are only particular traditions which can either witness to their truth, make temporary coalitions with other traditions, or become, in a once public but now technicized realm, merely particularist "interest groups" struggling with and against other equally particularist groups. As we will see below, there is no good reason to discourage either "witnessing" or "coalitions" in the public realm as long as these are not considered exhaustive options. However, there is every good reason for all witnessing groups and all coalition partners to be as deeply troubled about the loss of a public realm as any other thinker who still believes in its possibility-in-principle.[7] The departure of shared norms for reason and publicness may mean that reasonable argument may exit from the public realm. But the exit of "truth" is not the exit of "power"—as the quick contemporary slide from "witness" and "coalitions" to "interest groups" in the presently impoverished "public realm" starkly demonstrates.

The issue of publicness can be posed, therefore, in this way: Is it or is it not the case that, however particular in origin and expression any classic work of art or religion may be, its effects are nonetheless public? To shift the questions of art and religion (and, even, as suggested above, reason itself) away from origins to effects is a first step to providing a more adequate list of candidates for public discourse. My own work in the nature of "the classic" leads me to this conclusion.[8] For every classic work of art or religion is highly particular in both origin and expression yet deeply public in result. As reception-theory in modern hermeneutics attempts to show, even if we cannot agree on the *origins* of a classic work of art, we can still agree on its effects. Those effects can only be described as public, i.e., shared, open to all human beings. The effects of a classic work of art or a classic religious tradition are public as providing disclosive and transformative possibilities for all persons. Their publicness, indeed their truth, is precisely their disclosive and transformative reality. The spectrum of possible responses (of disclosure and transformation) to any classic varies widely: ranging, on one end of the spectrum, from a tentative sense of resonance to the other end where the experience is more appropriately described as a "shock of recognition." In *every* case along the whole spectrum, however, *some* disclosure-transformation, and thereby some truth, is in fact present—and present as communicable, shareable, public.[9]

If strictly positivist and instrumentalist notions of reason and publicness are alone allowed, then the possibility of the concrete experience of the truths of art and religion as truth-as-disclosure and transformation is, of course disallowed. Then, as the public realm itself becomes more and more scientized and technicized, art becomes marginalized and religion becomes privatized. But if—to employ classic Aristotelian terms—poetics and rhetoric are also allowed to make claims to truth (poetics through disclosure-transformation; rhetoric through persuasive argument, not fanciful ornamentation),[10] then the role of reason itself is properly expanded—and properly focused in its *de facto* effects, not its speculative "origins." As Stephen Toulmin has observed, the rediscovery of Aristotle's *Topics* is also a rediscovery of the claims to truth, to shareable, public meaning in rhetoric itself (and, by expansion of Toulmin's suggestion, in the poetics, ethics, politics and metaphysics). I do not pretend to have defended this expanded list of candidates for truth-claims in this brief "thought-experiment." Yet this much is, I believe, warranted even on this limited basis: the problem of the role of religion in the public realm needs, above all, to focus on analyzing a more comprehensive notion of reason itself and thereby of religion's own relationships to that more comprehensive role. One strategy for achieving that is to shift the major focus of the discussion away from origins to effects. In that shift, the role of any classic (and here the classics of art and religion are illuminating for the analagous nature of the classic models of reason itself) is the role of a phenomenon that is always particular in origin and expression yet always public in effect.

It is not the case, therefore, that our only alternatives are a positivist and instrumentalist definition of the public realm or a sheer chaos, a multiplicity of positions on publicness, meaning and truth sliding into the abyss of "power-politics" amidst competing interest-groups. It is the case that reason itself, however particular in origin and expression, is public in effect. And reason itself is comprehensive enough to include both argument (including de facto transcendental arguments) on the conditions for possibility of our common, shared, public discourse and conversation with all the classic expressions of the culture, including the religious classics.[11] Such a scenario, I believe, suggests the fuller meaning of an authentically public realm where argument and conversation are demanded of all participants. What this might mean more concretely for the present question of the possible role of religion in American culture I shall now try to address.

II

To produce public discourse is to provide reasons for one's assertions. To provide reasons is to render one's claims shareable, public. To provide reasons is to be willing to engage in argument. For argument is the most obvious form of public discourse. To engage in argument is to make claims and to give the warrants and backings for those claims.[12] Argument is not exhausted by the purely deductive procedures of the traditional syllogism nor by some contemporary narrow understandings of logic. To be reasonable is, however, to be logical. To be logical is to be coherent. To argue is to demand coherence. To argue is also to demand the kind of evidence appropriate to the subject matter under discussion. To argue is to engage—to defend and correct—one's assertions publicly by providing the appropriate evidence, warrants, backings, appropriate to the concrete subject-matter under discussion. Entailed by this commitment to public argument is the willingness also to render explicit the criteria appropriate to the subject-matter under discussion. Those criteria will prove to be, in any case where the question is other than one of coherence, criteria of relative adequacy—relative to the appropriate subject-matter and relative to the evidence presently available on this subject-matter. With this understanding of argument one can argue publicly not only over the appropriate means to achieve a particular end, but over the particular end itself. The structure of the argument because of the nature of the subject-matter must be more difficult, complex, and tentative on any question of ends. And yet, as argument, the discussion of ends and values is public, not private or preferential.

The move to explicit argument is the most obvious way to assure publicness. If there is a public realm, this means at least that there is a realm where argument is not merely allowed but demanded. This means, as well, that truth in the public realm will be fundamentally a matter of consensus—a consensus of the community of inquiry cognizant of and guided by the criteria and evidence of the particular subject-matter under discussion. A community of inquiry must be democratic, even radically egalitarian in the most fundamental sense:[13] the sense that no one is accorded privileged status in an argument, all are equal, all are bound to produce and yield to evidence, warrants, backings. The emerging consensus must be a consensus responsible to the best argument.

The first responsibility of the public realm is, therefore, the responsibility to give reasons, to provide arguments—to be public. Argument has traditionally been—and must remain—the primary candidate for publicness. And yet there is a second candidate as well—one related to, yet distinct from, argument itself. That candidate, as I suggested above, is the phenomenon of conversation. More exactly, conversation is a phenomenon which, in a general sense, is scarcely distinguishable from argument. This is so insofar as there is no genuine conversation unless the general criteria for argument are also observed: criteria of intelligibility (coherence), truth (warrants-evidence), right (moral integrity) and equality (mutual reciprocity).[14] These general criteria can serve, in fact, as de facto conditions of possibility for the presence or absence of both argument and conversation.

However, there are forms of conversation which, although responsible to these general criteria, are nonetheless also so distinctive in the kind of truth they attain for a possible consensus and so important for the public realm that they demand explicit treatment. I refer to the discussion above on the conversation with the classics of a culture.

A classic is a phenomenon whose excess and permanence of meaning resists definitive interpretation.[15] The classics of art and religion are phenomena whose truth-value is dependent upon their disclosive and transformative possibilities for their interpreters. This does not mean, to repeat, that the conversation with the classics can abandon the general criteria for publicness cited above. This does mean, however, that the concrete classics of art and religion are likely to manifest disclosive and transformative truths in a manner that is not reducible to the structure of our more usual arguments. Truth as disclosure-transformation is a concrete experience of truth, available in principle to all who will risk entering into conversation with the classics. Here, in sum, conversation means the entry by the interpreter into the to-and-fro movement of the questions and responses of the classic itself. The interpreter enters with some pre-understanding of those questions (e.g., religion). Nonetheless the interpreter is willing to risk that pre-understanding by noting the claim to attention of the classic.

That claim to attention may range across a whole spectrum from a tentative resonance to a shock of recognition.[16] The experience is one, primarily, of a reality that is important and true, and recognized in the disclosure to be so.

It is important to note that this modern hermeneutical understanding of conversation does not involve either a purely autonomous text or a purely passive recipient-interpreter. The central key to a conversation with a classic is neither the text nor the interpreter but the to-and-fro movement between them. The central moment of truth for this conversation with the classics of art and religion is the moment of disclosure-transformation that *can* occur when the interpreter risks addressing (and thereby entering into genuine conversation with) the claim to attention of the classic. Precisely as conversation, this interaction is shared, shareable, public. Precisely as the result of conversation, the disclosure-transformation is a public candidate for possible consensus in the public realm.

If we are really engaged with a classic (and not a period-piece) this means that the interpretation-as-conversation will necessarily be a different interpretation than that of its original author or its original audience. It is the effect that remains public, not the origin. For, as Gadamer correctly observes, insofar as we understand at all, we understand differently (than the original author). The classics of any culture have always been considered phenomena in the public realm precisely through their disclosive and transformative shareable possibilities. Those possibilities come to us through the more elusive, but no less real, form of a conversation than through the more usual form of "argument." But once those possibilities come, they come as candidates for consensus for the entire community— candidates whose poetic (as distinct from both analytical and rhetorical) forms is the impact of a truth-as disclosure, not a truth as the explicit conclusion of an argument.

Since those disclosures come to us, they do not come to

passive recipients interested only in reconstructing their origins. The classics appear with a claim to disclosure, a claim to our attention as *ours*—i.e., as those willing to enter into conversation with them. As conversation-*partners* we must remain open to the risk of a retrieval of their disclosures. As *conversation*-partners, we must remain equally open to any necessary critique or suspicion of the errors and systematic distortions also possibly present in them and in the history of their effects.[17] Every great work of civilization, as Walter Benjamin justly observed, is also a work of barbarism. Every great classic, every classic tradition needs both retrieval and critique-suspicion. Every classic needs continuing conversation by the community constituted by its history of effects. The community of inquiry, grounded in public argument, thereby expands to become as well the community of interpretation of the classics, grounded in the general rules for conversation and argument alike and grounded as well in the particular demands and risks of a genuine conversation with the disclosive claim to attention of every classic. Both communities are public; both are grounded in consensus.

The community of interpretation of the classics is also responsible for rendering explicit its criteria of relative adequacy for good, bad, better (more adequate) readings of the classics. Any personal response to the disclosive power of the classic is indeed highly personal in experience. But once that experience is expressed, it becomes a public concern—subject to the rules for publicness of the entire community of inquiry and interpretation. It is unlikely, for example, that the same response to the classics of a particular religious tradition will be found among both participants in (believers in) that tradition and others interpreting that tradition from "outside." But if the religious classics of any particular tradition are genuine classics, then they will also provide public, disclosive possibilities to all.

III

In American culture,[18] for example, the phenomenon once named "Atheists for Niebuhr" is worth puzzling about. The fact is that Reinhold Niebuhr's interpretation of the disclosive and transformative power of the Christian symbols of sin-grace provided public resources for understanding aspects of our common, shared life even for those who did not share Niebuhr's own explicitly Christian faith. This phenomenon of "atheists for Niebuhr" is not, therefore, as paradoxical as it at first seems. Insofar as there exists a full spectrum of possible responses to the disclosive power of any classic, shareability or publicness is achieved across the entire spectrum of responses despite all other differences in response. Anyone who both experiences and expresses an interpretation of any disclosure of any classic thereby shares that possibility with *all* others—whether those "others" prove to be ones for whom a full "shock of recognition" (as, religiously, "faith") has occurred or those for whom only some resonance has happened. On this reading, both the classics of art and the classics of religion are candidates for the public realm. It is not the case that only "believers in" a particular classic (i.e., those who have experienced a full shock of recognition) can interpret these classics properly, publicly. All members of the community of interpretation can and should risk interpreting them: interpreting them precisely to see if they provide some disclosive and transformative possibility for the public realm itself. To marginalize art and to privatize religion is to encourage the drift to scientize and technicize the public realm itself. To marginalize art and to privatize religion is to narrow the comprehensive notion of reason itself. For the consensus of the community of inquiry would contradict its own norms by allowing for every argument save the argument that the same criteria for reasonable argument (intelligibility, truth, rightness, mutual reciprocity) are also to be found in every genuine conversation—including any conversation with the disclosive and transformative truths of the classics of art and religion. A public realm is public and true because grounded in consensus. The public realm, the community of consensus, is both a community of inquiry (argument) and a community of interpretation (conversation with the classics).

Both communities, moreover, have survived in the two classic traditions of the American experiment itself. The American Enlightenment tradition (best represented in Jefferson) is fundamentally a tradition of reason based on argument in the broad sense described above. And the second founding tradition, the Puritan covenantal tradition, is, like all religious traditions, grounded in conversation with particular religious classics.

The Enlightenment tradition defines the classic American attempt at a public realm grounded in a rationality open to all, grounded therefore in a consensus appropriate to every community of inquiry. The Puritan covenantal tradition defines the classic American attempt to engage in a genuine conversation with the classics of both religion and art (recall Jonathan Edwards). Thereby does the American community of reason, inquiry, argument also become a covenanting community of interpretation of shared classic symbols. Insofar as the American experiment was guided by these two classic traditions, it developed a public realm that was both a community of inquiry (argument) and a community of interpretation (conversation with the classic religious and artistic symbols). The more comprehensive notion of reason implicit in the American Enlightenment notion of argument freed that Enlightenment tradition to open, initially with Madison, classically in a later period with Lincoln, to conversation with the principal religious and artistic classics as well. The conversational model of truth as disclosure implicit in the Puritan tradition empowered its trajectory—one that moves from Edwards through Emerson to James, Dewey, and Royce—to include a peculiarly American aesthetic understanding of ethics and an admission, in principle, of both art and religion as candidates for disclosive possibilities in the public realm.

The most original (and clearly the classic) American tradition of philosophy—the pragmatic tradition—is one that continued, in various ways, these two classic strands: the Enlightenment comprehensive notion of reason-as-argument in Jefferson became the explicitly consensus theory of truth for the community of inquiry and the democratic ethos in Peirce and Dewey; the Puritan tradition, with its implicitly disclosive notion of truth-as-interpretation of the classics in Edwards, Lincoln (on the ethos of society) and Emerson (on the ethos of nature) became the explicitly community-of-interpretation position in Royce.

The list of candidates for models of reason has expanded, to be sure, beyond Jefferson's or even Dewey's and Peirce's own models. But the comprehensive notions of reason and argument which they defended in their day remain the classic American resources for recovering a public realm grounded in the consensus of a community of inquiry become a democratic polity. The dialectic of the American Enlightenment may have proved more dialectical than either Jefferson or Dewey foresaw. But the route from Enlightenment reason to sheer technique and ever narrower notions of reason cannot be laid to their account. They defended argument, reason, publicness in a comprehensive sense. They never defended reason as pure technique or positivist verification.

The list of candidates of religious and artistic classics has also expanded beyond the earlier Puritan beginning. Yet the implicit appeal to the model of conversation in the Puritan notion of covenant can, in principle, break that earlier hegemony without abandoning that heritage. For pluralism here fundamentally means that the list of American artistic and religious classics has expanded to the point where the Puritan classics are now joined by others as well (black, native American, Catholic, Jewish, southern, feminist, etc.). All are candidates for the public realm. All need, as much as the Enlightenment and pragmatic models of reason, conversation that includes both retrieval and critique-suspicion.

Insofar as one defends argument and conversation, one defends a public realm. Insofar as one allows argument to be narrowed to scientistic and technological models, one abandons the classic American Enlightenment tradition of "civic discourse" and its comprehensive notion of reason. Insofar as one shuns conversations with the classics to the margins of the society or the privacy of an individual's heart or even to the wider privacy of a witnessing community quickly become one more "reservation of the spirit," one abandons the classic American convenantal tradition grounded in a model of conversation with the classics. Consensus is the hope of the public realm. But consensus prevails as a claim to truth and not merely a survey of interests when consensus lives in an arguing community of inquiry and a conversing community of interpretation. The two classic traditions of the American experiment with a public realm suggest as much. More importantly, both demand no less of all their later descendants.

Notes

1. For the question of rationality, see *Rationality Today: La Rationalité Aujourd' Hui*, ed. Theodore F. Geraets (Ottawa: The University of Ottawa Press, 1979); see also Richard Sennett, *The Fall of Public Man* (New York: Knopf, 1977).

2. For representative works, see Thomas Kuhn, *The Structure*

of Scientific Revolutions (Chicago: University of Chicago, 1970); Stephen Toulmin, *The Uses of Argument* (Cambridge: Cambridge University Press, 1958); Hilary Putnam, *Reason, Truth and History* (Cambridge: Cambridge University Press, 1981).

3. Richard Rorty, *Philosophy and the Mirror of Nature* (Princeton: Princeton University Press, 1979); Paul Feyerabend, *Against Method* (London: Dersen, 1978).

4. See also Richard J. Bernstein, *Beyond Objectivism and Relativism: Science, Hermeneutics and Praxis* (Philadelphia: University of Pennsylvania Press, 1983).

5. Alasdair MacIntyre, *After Virtue* (Notre Dame: University of Notre Dame Press, 1981).

6. See the discussion in Christopher Norris, *Deconstruction: Theory and Practice* (London: Methuen, 1982).

7. See William Sullivan, *Reconstructing Public Philosophy* (Berkeley: University of California, 1982); *Hannah Arendt: The Recovery of the Public World*, ed. Melvin A. Hill (New York: St. Martin's Press, 1979).

8. See David Tracy, *The Analogical Imagination: Christian Theology and the Culture of Pluralism* (New York: Crossroad, 1981), pp. 99–154.

9. For a defense of this, see my forthcoming book, *Plurality and Ambiguity: Interpretation and Religion* (New York: Seabury-Winston, 1986).

10. For a good example of neo-Aristotelian criticism, see *Critics and Criticism*, ed. R.S. Crane (Chicago: University of Chicago Press, 1952).

11. See Hans-Georg Gadamer, *Truth and Method* (New York: Seabury, 1975) on conversation and the classics.

12. On argument, see Stephen Toulmin, *The Uses of Argument*, *op. cit.*

13. See John Dewey, "Creative Democracy—The Task Before Us," in *Classic American Philosophers*, ed. Max Fisch (New York: Appleton-Century Crofts, 1951).

14. Jürgen Habermas, *Communication and the Evolution of Society* (Boston: Beacon Press, 1979).

15. See *The Analogical Imagination*, *op. cit.*, pp. 99–154.

16. Hans Robert Jauss, *Toward an Aesthetic of Reception* (Minneapolis: University of Minnesota Press, 1982).

17. Paul Ricoeur, "Ethics and Culture," in *Political and Social Essays*, ed. David Stewart and Joseph Bien (Athens: Ohio University Press, 1974).

18. The following section makes no pretenses to a full-fledged historical analysis; indeed, it is best read as a "thought-experiment" on the most familiar texts and thinkers of the American tradition in the light of the argument of the first two sections. I hope to develop the present speculations in a fuller historical form in a book; in the meantime, it seems best to leave them in their present "thought-experiment" state and, therefore, without footnotes.

Social Contract or a
Public Covenant?

ROBIN W. LOVIN

RELIGIOUS LANGUAGE IS A PERVASIVE FEATURE of our public life, but a canny observer soon notes that it is usually a language of legitimation, not a language of persuasion. Whether
it comes in the form of "Good night and God bless you," at the
close of a presidential address, or the recollection of the prophets' cry for justice at a protest rally, religious language enters
public speech when the speaker has some confidence that the
audience already agrees. The speakers may call for stability or
change, for freedom, order, or justice, but they will seldom call
for it in God's name until they are sure that they have enlisted
their hearers' self-interest on other grounds.

The situation is plain enough, but we do not often ask
why it is so, and when we do ask, the reasons given are usually
inadequate. What I want to suggest is that the limitations we
put on religious ideas in public discussion derive from our limited ideas about politics, not from the limitations of religion.
These limits are neither the result of some recent trend toward
secularism, nor a reflection of Jeffersonian fears of sectarian
faction. If Jefferson enters into the matter at all, it is because

the limits are a reflection of some ideas about politics that were common in the eighteenth century and that are still a part of our political institutions because the ideas were fixed in the minds of the men who made the institutions.

Attempts to explain the constraints on religion in public life often point to an implicit code of conduct that bans religious discussion as divisive or discourteous. Offering religious reasons for public action is a particularistic appeal that excludes some members of the public and may make them feel inferior.[1] A more philosophical explanation suggests that since propositions about God's will or God's action can only be verified by those who share the belief in question, the persuasive force of religious language ends at the boundaries of the sanctuary. In a culture that is increasingly secular, and in which religious beliefs are remarkably diverse, talk about what God does or wants us to do has meaning only for those who happen already to agree with it.[2] What these sociological and philosophical explanations have in common is that they locate the problem in religion. Religious appeals must be limited in public discussion because of peculiar characteristics of religious language that render it socially divisive, inflammatory, or unverifiable. Religious language must be limited to a legitimating or hortatory role in public life because that is the only way we can be sure we have a public understanding of what it means.

Upon reflection, however, this characterization of religious language is itself peculiar. Some religious propositions may, indeed, make claims about God and God's will that no one can evaluate on the basis of common human experiences, but in general John E. Smith's observation is apt: every alleged experience of God is at the same time an experience of something else.[3] Religious language may be and commonly is about the persistent features of human life, about human needs, and about what persons can expect in their interactions with each other, quite as much as it is about God. The veracity of these particular claims may be disputed. One may even question whether it is possible to draw general conclusions about "human nature" at all. These are not, however, problems unique to religious language. They trouble every attempt to establish a general idea about human experience that could be used to criticize the specific plans and choices that persons might make.

FROM COVENANT TO CONTRACT

These philosophical problems became entangled with American political life very early in our history. The social contract theories that prevailed in Britain and America in the eighteenth century had a problem explaining how persons could arrive at general ideas about human nature, and they found it particularly difficult to explain how such a general idea could override the specific wants of an individual. What I suggest in this essay, then, is that some of the limitations we put on religion in public discussions can be traced to some problems in English thought at the time our institutions and national attitudes were being formed. There are, of course, some genuinely new problems for religion in our public life today, but some of the most important ones are not new at all. They begin with what happened to our ideas about society in the little more than a century and a half from the first settlement of New England to the adoption of the Federal Constitution.

Perhaps the most important religious idea in old and New England at the beginning of that time period was the idea of a covenant society, for that was what the early Puritans wanted to build all over old England, and that was what their successors tried to establish in their plantations in North America. A covenant idea of society emerges when people are not content to see their relations to one another simply in terms of natural ties such as kinship, marriage relations, or the accidents of being born in the same village, or speaking the same language, or living under the same ruler. A covenant society is one in which the members are bound together by choice, by mutual commitment, more than by chance. A covenant society is one in which the members see their moral obligations as growing out of this commitment, so that they not only hold their neighbors to a higher standard of conduct than they might if they were just thrown together at random; they expect more of themselves and they acknowledge that others who share in the covenant have a right to examine and criticize their behavior. Above all, the covenant creates this sense of mutual accountability not only to one another, but before God. It is not the moral health of each individual which is under scrutiny, but the righteousness or waywardness of the whole society. This sense that there is a common good, a well-being of the whole society that cannot be measured just by summing up the achievements and faults of all the individuals in it, is crucial to the covenant idea.

The Puritan covenant was modeled, obviously, on the covenant between God and Israel which dominates the political thought of the Hebrew Scriptures. It owes much, too, to the images of early Christian community that appear in Acts and in the letters of Paul in the New Testament. There, mutual help in material need and mutual criticism in moral terms go hand in hand. The sense of commitment and accountability that was basic to the community created a kind of moral equality among the people, and this moral equality balanced out their obvious inequalities in terms of birth, achievement, wealth, and social status. It is possible to criticize these idyllic pictures of the Davidic kingdom and their early Church, but the point is that the Puritans believed it was like that, and what they believed was what they tried to re-create in their own place and time.

For the founders of Massachusetts Bay, the new world was supposed to provide what the old could not—a place where this covenant could be lived out in practice. John Winthrop's famous speech to the colonists anchored in Massachusetts Bay makes the point:

> We must not content ourselves with usual ordinary means. Whatsoever we did or ought to have done when we lived in England, the same must we do and more also where we go. That which the most in their churches maintain as a truth in profession only, we must bring into familiar and constant practice. As in this duty of love, we must love brotherly without dissimulation. We must love one another with a pure heart. Fervently we must bear one another's burdens. We must not look only on our own things, but also on the things of our brethren.[4]

The connection between religion and public life is here quite straightforward. Public life is where religion is put into practice.

By the time of the Revolution, however, a new, less direct way of speaking had become dominant. What happened was not so much that people turned against the covenant idea as that they found it increasingly difficult to understand. At the same time that the Massachusetts Bay settlers were pledging themselves to be good and to do right in a covenant of mutual accountability, the English philosophers who shaped the thought of the next generation were discovering that it is, after all, very hard to explain just how we know what we ought to be trying to be and to do.

There was in the philosophy of the time a growing awareness of the individuality and diversity of human aims and desires. Aristotle's old dictum that man is a rational animal who can control the passions in the interest of some natural standard of virtue began to give way to a more empirical observation of what people do, in fact, desire and pursue. What they desire and pursue, it seemed to observers at the time, was nothing so simple as a rational ideal. Indeed, as Hobbes noticed, they seemed to desire all kinds of things, first this and then that, in no special order, and without any final goal in mind.[5]

What happened between the founding of the Massachusetts Bay Colony in 1630 and the Constitutional Convention of 1789 must be understood in light of this sweeping intellectual change on both sides of the Atlantic. We may think of this as the Age of Reason, but it was also a time in which people were deeply impressed with the individualism of human subjectivity.

The conclusions drawn from this were unlikely conclusions for an age of reason, but philosophers drew them nonetheless. Reason, said the empiricist philosophers of the eighteenth century, is the servant of the passions. Reason helps us to choose the best means to get what we want. Reason may keep us from pursuing our desires in ways that are apt to do us harm, but reason does not choose the goals that we pursue. If we want to discuss matters rationally, the Age of Reason suggested, we would do well to keep the talk within fairly narrow bounds. Reason can help us to choose the best means to reach an end that we already want, but it cannot choose the ends for us. Above all, the philosophers added, there is no way that your reason can penetrate my desire and no basis for you to say that I should not want what I want.

Obviously, this new philosophy posed problems for the covenant community. The idea of commitment to a community that would engage in mutual criticism of one another's choices now seemed a bit strange. The idea that a community should encourage, exhort, and perhaps even coerce its members to live up to the possibilities in human nature; the idea that a community should organize itself to achieve a common good; the idea that each member would be accountable for how well the whole community did—all those notions now became problematic, and not just because some people did not like the particular form that the covenant took in Puritanism. The covenant community began to seem strange because the new philosophy implied that there could be no way to talk rationally about the choices and criticisms that community wanted to make.

Increasingly, therefore, the talk in English and American public life was not of *covenant*, but of *contract*. While the words initially meant much the same thing, and were used interchangeably by Hobbes and other early modern political writers, it becomes clear as the tradition develops that a social contract is a quite different way to organize a society.[6]

The contract that Hobbes and Locke had in mind was a commitment made for quite definite purposes. One accepts the constraints of life in society, not because that commitment makes one a better person or improves the quality of one's goals and aims. One accepts the constraints because a certain amount of mutual restraint, reason suggests, is the only way that we will be able to live together at all. In a world where we are all continuously engaged in the pursuit of essentially irrational desires, our rational capacity to make agreements with one another does not necessarily bring unanimity to our choices, but it does give some order and predictability to public life. That in turn will allow us as individuals to lay plans to pursue our goals more effectively.

THE LIMITS OF THE SOCIAL CONTRACT

Clearly, then, this contractarian view of public life was drawn to fit the limits imposed by the new, individualized empiricist philosophy. If we can argue rationally only over means to ends, then public debate is a matter of identifying those minimal achievements which turn out, happily, to be means to everybody's ends in the long run. Once we can demonstrate that every human project requires some protection by the law, or that we must expect people to keep their agreements if we are to do anything at all, we have a basis for establishing public expectations that do not require us to go into the difficult, and perhaps impossible, business of scrutinizing, criticizing, and correcting the aims that individuals happen to have. Public discussion focuses on how a person is to get what he or she wants with minimal intrusions upon the desires of others. What a person ought to want is not open to examination.

Public life is no longer thought of as a place to learn and practice virtue. Virtues, if we are to have them at all, must be inculcated in the home, or the church, or perhaps in the understandings that provide a code of decent professional conduct for lawyers, scholars, bankers, and so forth. Public life does not so much require virtue as it requires the restraint of vice.

This brief account of the contractarian social theory that came to dominate eighteenth century English liberalism is, of course, sketchy in some places and overdrawn in others, but one can recognize in it some themes that still are heard in Anglo-American political philosophy. John Rawls' insistence that a theory of justice should be designed to protect *any* rational plan of life and should not choose between the different goods that free and equal citizens may desire owes much to this eighteenth century theory,[7] as does the rigorous separation of law and morals in H.L.A. Hart's theory of law.[8] Above all, the general idea that Americans have about what is and is not fit material for public debate derives from this origin. We are a people who insist that the rules of civility include an avoidance of unnecessary and unresolvable arguments. Religion, values, virtues, and goals belong in the realm of private conversation, reflection, and persuasion, while the public forum concerns itself with the limited range of issues on which we have to agree.

Notice, then, that the reason for this transition from covenant to contract theory was not primarily theological. It was not that ideas about religion changed and led the pastors and preachers to give up on the idea of a covenantal community. What changed were ideas about knowledge. The reduced scope of discussion in public life followed from an epistemological theory that we have no way to know good and bad in human aims, no normative concept of human nature, and no way to criticize social arrangements apart from the desires of those who happen to be a part of them. Once those constraints were widely accepted, those who were concerned with political life set about to revise the rules to provide for a debate that would turn on what we can know.

Clearly, that strategy was not without its values. Shifting public attention from the criticism of human ends to the rational choice of means that everyone could use did avoid some nasty civil conflicts, and it probably encouraged the emergence of a more pluralistic society that offered its people a greater range of real options for their lives.

Nevertheless, this view of the public forum has its own limitations, as some Americans discovered before the Civil War when they wanted to criticize the injustice of a fugitive slave law that was procedurally correct and perfectly legal. In that instance, and others like it, people returned to language about "inalienable rights" or a "higher law" that overrules some of our specific laws and policies. The concepts are vague, to be sure, but there are points in our thinking about human life in society at which it is absolutely necessary to fall back on them.[9] The insistence that some contracts are unworthy of human beings and some projects are destructive of an essential human nature are appeals that we will not forego. We hesitate, properly, before invoking those concepts. Not every public issue is a question of human rights, and not every political question can be settled by natural law. But we ought also to work on clarifying those concepts and applying them where they do belong, and we certainly should not hesitate to do so because the ideas are incompatible with an individualized eighteenth century psychology that has long been obsolete.

OPEN QUESTIONS AND A PUBLIC COVENANT

We began this discussion with the suggestion that the limitations on religion in public, political discussions in America arise more from problems in our politics than from inherent limitations in religion. Those problems should now be more evident, and perhaps, too, the outlines of a solution have begun to emerge.

The key to the renewal of public discourse is a new attentiveness to the normative dimensions of our ideas of human nature. Although we have tried to organize our politics without this discussion, it seems increasingly clear that there are some questions that cannot be answered without a decision about how human beings are meant to live and what they require from one another to flourish in a human society. In that discussion, religion has a substantive, and not merely hortatory, part to play. Religion is certainly not the only source of ideas for this discussion, but all religions offer something to it. Indeed, religious communities hardly know what to say at all, if they cannot articulate their vision of the good life for persons. That is why religion has so little to contribute in the contractarian setting where that discussion is ruled out in advance.

However that discussion might develop in public life today, it surely will reintroduce some dimensions of the covenant of mutual accountability and mutual criticism that prevailed in the politics of early New England. Normative discussions of human nature cannot take individual life plans for granted. What I want for myself must be measured against a standard of what it means to be fully human. I can be asked to justify the person I want to become, and not merely means I use to do it. At the same time, we have to find a standard for measuring society's achievements that is more penetrating than asking how well the society satisfies individual wants. The idea of the common good, which in the eighteenth century was reduced to the sum of our individual goods, can again be a subject for public discussion. A view of public life that begins with an understanding of human nature informed by religious traditions would thus recapture much of the sense of mutual accountability and commitment to a common project that characterized the ideal of a covenant society in Puritanism.

Of course, in a pluralistic and technological age, no workable social vision can be simply identical with the Puritan covenant. John Winthrop, living in a small colony on the edge of a primeval forest, could deal with diversity simply by excluding anyone who was different. That option is neither possible nor desirable for us. Hence the need to stress that a covenant for our society must be a *public* covenant.

Stating a religious vision of human fulfillment does not end discussion of human nature; it begins it. As David Tracy's essay in this volume indicates, the resulting discussion must be public in the sense that religious traditions which press their insights into human needs and human nature must do so in terms that can make sense to anyone, including those who disagree and those who refuse to share the theological starting point.

A public covenant requires, too, that we recognize the importance of open questions. In a contractarian system, which tries to resolve only the questions that are critical for public order, every question has to be resolved somehow. In the end, if consensus fails, you take a vote. Part of the contract is that everybody agrees to abide by the majority decision. Unfortunately, we have become so accustomed to that way of settling unresolved issues that we begin to mistake this way of dealing with the lack of agreement for a way of finding answers. Issues like women's rights, the question of when life begins, or the acceptability of public religious expressions are simply to be put to a vote, and the winner takes all.

Questions about human needs and human nature, however, do not lend themselves to procedural solutions. Answers, when answers are available, emerge out of long public discussion, out of a pattern of statement, persuasion, restatement, and modification, often over several generations. At any point in that process, there will be many questions that simply cannot be answered. There will be questions that remain open. Public discussion on these matters may not immediately result in satisfactory policy choices, but over the long run it is such discussions that shape the solutions.

So the idea of a public covenant is just the opposite of a promise of easy answers, drawn from some authoritative religious source. The public covenant requires us to make our religious authorities comprehensible and persuasive, and it requires us to increase our patience for dealing with open questions in public forums.

Among these open questions, of course, is the question of the public covenant itself. It would be foolish to suppose that at some point in the future such a document could be drawn up and adopted. A public covenant comes into being when people in the public start to take its questions seriously. A public covenant exists to the extent that people in discussion measure the goals and performances of public policy against a normative idea of human nature and to the extent that they hold themselves open and accountable to the same scrutiny. The idea of a public covenant in a pluralistic society depends in part on theories about what we can know and how we can explain the truths of our faith. Whether that covenant will exist, however, is a decision that we make in practice, in the problems we bring to public discussion and the ways we are willing to enter into it.

Notes

1. John Murray Cuddihy, *No Offense* (New York: Seabury Press, 1978). Cuddihy suggests that the public "civility" which avoids religious appeals originates in a Protestant cultural hegemony that tries to prevent others from raising arguments that might call it into question.

2. Kai Nielsen, "Some Remarks on the Independence of Morality from Religion," in Ian T. Ramsey, ed., *Christian Ethics and Contemporary Philosophy* (New York: Macmillan, 1966), pp. 140–42.

3. John E. Smith, *Experience and God* (New York: Oxford University Press, 1968), p. 52.

4. John Winthrop, "A Model of Christian Charity," in Edmund S. Morgan, ed., *Puritan Political Ideas: 1558–1794* (Indianapolis: Bobbs-Merrill Co., 1965), pp. 90–91. Spelling and punctuation have been modernized.

5. Thomas Hobbes, *Leviathan*, ed. C.B. Macpherson (Harmondsworth: Penguin Books, 1968), pp. 160–61.

6. These differences have been studied especially in H. Richard Niebuhr, "The Idea of Covenant and American Democracy," *Church History* 23 (1954): 126–35; and in Douglas Sturm, "Corporations, Constitutions, and Covenants: On Forms of Human Relation and the Problem of Legitimacy," *Journal of the American Academy of Religion* 41 (1973), 331–54.

7. John Rawls, *A Theory of Justice* (Cambridge, Mass.: Harvard University Press, 1971).

8. H.L.A. Hart, *The Concept of Law* (Oxford: Oxford University Press, 1961).

9. Archibald Cox, *The Role of the Supreme Court in American Government* (New York: Oxford University Press, 1976), pp. 111–12.

A Sort of Republican Banquet

MARTIN E. MARTY

IN LATE SPRING OF 1831 two young French noblemen spent nine days observing Sing Sing prison in New York. After Sunday worship one of them, Gustave de Beaumont, wrote a letter to his mother. Each week, he reported, a minister belonging to a different communion preached to the captives. "All the prisoners attend the service together, without perhaps knowing the difference between the sects to which their preachers belong. If they don't, so much the better," he mused. But if they do know the difference, "they must find themselves much embarrassed to choose between the various cults the best and only true one."

From views of the hard benches at Sing Sing, Beaumont leaped in imagination to conclude that nothing was more common in America than "indifference toward the nature of religions." Yet, he continued, this indifference did not "eliminate the religious fervour of each for the cult he has chosen." The writer was puzzled over what he called "this extreme tolerance on the one hand toward religions in general—on the other this considerable zeal of each individual for his own religion." How could "a lively and sincere faith . . . get on with such a perfect toleration?" How could a person have "equal respect for religions whose dogmas differ?" What real influence on the moral conduct of the Americans, he wondered, "can be exercised by their religious spirit, whose outward manifestations, at least, are undeniable. Would it not be from their outward show of religion that there is more breadth than depth in it?"[1]

Upon landing in America that May, Beaumont's better-known colleague, Alexis de Tocqueville, asked an instant question: "How can the variety of sects not breed indifference, if not externally, then at least within? That is what remains to be known."[2] He, too, found at Sing Sing a "pretended toleration that had to be nothing else than good round indifference."[3]

The two visitors carried their questions and their prejudices with them on the road. Congressman John Canfield Spencer, at his summer home in upstate New York, gave them the popular defensive explanation for the tolerance they found as he cited "the extreme division of sects (which is almost without limits). If there were but two religions, we should cut each other's throats. But no sect having the majority, all have need of tolerance."[4] Voltaire had earlier voiced just such a notion about England, and James Madison later restated it for America, where, he said, security for civil and religious rights consisted "in the multiplicity of interests . . . and . . . the multiplicity of sects."[5]

Spencer then pushed on to a second "generally accepted opinion" which held that "some sort of religion is necessary to man in society, the more so the freer he is."[6] In his classic *Democracy in America*, Tocqueville showed how he here agreed with the attorney. Instinctive Ciceronians that they were, he and Spencer thought that a republic needed a *consensus juris*, a profound agreement about values undergirding law and society. Cicero had gone even further: "Each commonwealth has its own religion, and we have ours" ("Sua cuique civitati religio est, nostra nobis" [*Pro flacco* 2:8]).[7] The sects, in their understanding, had to be tolerant of each other for the sake of consensus.

On July 22, soon after the pair of Frenchmen arrived at the "fine American village" of Detroit, Father Gabriel Richard provided a third rationale for American tolerance. This former Congressman, a Catholic elected by Protestants, argued that citizens knew how to bracket their sectarianism in order to show tolerance: "Nobody asks you *of what religion you are, but if you can do the job*."[8] Yet Americans demanded some sort of religion from everybody. In Maryland that autumn Richard Spring Stewart argued that the belief of Americans was sincere, but their competitive churches did exert social pressure on people to choose one or another among them. Unbelief itself was not then socially permissible. "Public opinion," Stewart added, "accomplishes with us what the Inquisition was never able to do."[9] The sober French visitors shared this public concern for religion because they thought it necessary for "the moral conduct of the Americans," or for what I prefer to call social or public morale.[10]

The tolerance coupled with indifference that they both wanted to find and then seemed frightened to encounter blinded Beaumont and Tocqueville to the raw intolerance that still blighted the United States. They missed much by tending to stay close to look-alike people of old Protestant stock who had not yet headed out in full array on a nativist crusade against Catholics. Tocqueville did find the handful of American Catholics taking advantage of the tolerance that their former adversaries showed them while they themselves remained, as he put it, "still at bottom as intolerant as they have ever been, as intolerant in a word as people who believe."[11] True belief, in his mind, allowed for no tolerance.

Visitors who found as little conflict between sects as did Beaumont and Tocqueville were clearly out of physical range of noisy frontier Methodist and Baptist revivalists who, with larynxes and fists alike, competed for souls. They could not know, for example, that also in New York at that time a new group called the Mormons was gathering; they would soon be victims of persecution. They overlooked the ways plantation owners then dishonored black slave religion and kept the slaves from freely congregating. Yet even they reported on their glimpses of sectarian spite. While swatting mosquitoes at Saginaw in Michigan, in a "corner of the earth unknown to the world," Tocqueville counted six conflicting religions. He noted formidably immobile and absolutely dogmatic Catholics, religiously anarchic Protestants, and ancient pagans there battling for that earth. In the midst of the wretchedness of solitude and the troubles of the present, he heard the Lutheran condemn the Calvinist to eternal fire and the Calvinist the Unitarian, while the Catholic embraced them all in a common condemnation. The more tolerant Indian, in his rude faith, merely exiled his European brother from the happy hunting ground he had reserved for himself.[12] The next winter, in a southern town, a diplomat friend named Joel Roberts Poinsett agreed with Tocqueville that all of these groups would burn each other "if the civil power was given to any of those persuasions. There is always deep hatred between them."[13]

Not for their glimpses of intolerance, but for their perplexities over the character of tolerance, do later generations remember Beaumont and Tocqueville on American religion. They were right to stress how, as moderns, Americans "must choose" a sect because their religion no longer came with the territory, nor was it passed along with the genes. Second, people were truly fervent and zealous in loyalty to their own sects in those days. This they still are, and they prove it by fighting not between church bodies but within and over them. Parties in each denomination fight for control with a passion and finesse that proves the point of John Dewey: people "do not shoot because targets exist, but they set up targets in order that throwing and shooting may be more effective and significant."[14] Thus they would rather fight than switch; and many never did shift loyalties, despite a tradition of constant prophecies by observers who thought that mobile and intermarrying Americans would casually break denominational ties.

It is their third theme, that tolerance in the United States had to be born only of ignorance, indifference, and superficiality, that has misled succeeding observers, including myself when young, more than any other statement they made on the subject. I propose to challenge their notion and to supplant it with other explanations for American attitudes. Beaumont and Tocqueville came by their prejudices on this subject naturally. In Europe, official Catholicism always had opposed tolerance and inspired a horror of indifference even among those who, like Tocqueville, were lapsed members. For classical Protestants, the Reverend Nathaniel Ward in Massachusetts expressed the imported and enduring attitude. Ward derided the English people when he first sniffed among them the dangerous signals of friendliness across sectarian lines. "He that is willing to tolerate any Religion, or discrepant way of Religion, besides his own, unless it be in matters merely indifferent, either doubts of his own, or is not sincere in it."[15] To this day, taunters like to suggest that the really religious are those who believe enough to be fanatic and intolerant.

Americans, on these historic terms, were damned if they did show intolerance, because it led to the bloodshed of holy wars, and damned if they did not, because then they looked indifferent and superficial. Now, while it is true that religion did intensify some of the most savage conflicts in national history, including the war over slavery, sectarian strife itself left few corpses. As for the charge of superficiality, it would be difficult if not impossible to prove that the Americans were less profound in religion than the European common people against whom visitors compared them.[16] Between these two

sets of damns, however, citizens improvised a third way,
which the author of *Democracy in America* helped cause later observers to overlook. In this context, Perry Miller thought that
Tocqueville's pages on religion were "probably the least perceptive he ever wrote," because his "Gallic logic failed to en-
compass the spectacle of American irrationality."[17] But was
Miller here his usual perceptive self? I shall contribute to on-
going debates by challenging the charges of both simple indif-
ferentism and irrationality.

All those who study American religion and not merely religion in America have to join United States citizens in wres-
tling with the classic and here central problem of "the one and
the many." The great philosophical jouster with this problem,
William James, once provided an image for it that grew out of
an analogy to a political idea. Since analogy works both ways,
I shall carry his back to its source to offer an image that is designed to replace those of the sullenly tolerant inmates at Sing
Sing and the swatting sectarians around Saginaw. In a passage
written to counter absolutism in philosophy, William James
once asked a question that applies as well against exclusivism
in religion: "Why may not the world be a sort of republican
banquet . . . where all the qualities of being respect one another's personal sacredness, yet sit at the common table of
space and time?"[18]

William James, of course, was at the time busying himself
with apparently contradictory qualities of being, while we are
depicting apparently contradictory sectarian positions or, better, groups, that were forced to sit at a metaphoric common
table. They were able to do so most creatively when they began to show "respect for one another's personal sacredness."
The republican image is appropriate for the American scene.
Rich and diverse as it was, it still filled up with so many conflicting kinds of peoples and sects that they were compelled to
devise a compact of mutual tolerance, unless they wanted to

repeat unproductive ways determined by the old laws of the religious jungle. Forced thus to come to terms with each other, they developed what Abraham Lincoln called "bonds of affection" and "mystic chords of memory" because of common experiences of a sort that were denied their ancestors.[19]

The beginnings of tolerance, then, grew out of empathy born of firmness, not superficiality. Gabriel Marcel has remarked that tolerance cannot be manifest before intolerance; "tolerance is not primitive." It is "ultimately the negation of a negation, a counter-intolerance. . . . The more it is tied to a state of weakness, the less it is itself, the less it is tolerance." To the extent that I am aware of sticking to my opinion, I can conceive the opinion of another "to be worthy just because of the intense conviction with which he holds it; it may be that my awareness of my own conviction is somehow my guarantee of the worth of his." Mutual understanding, in that case, grounds itself not in doubt or skepticism, says Marcel, but in transcendence, where respect for "one another's personal sacredness" takes shape.[20]

Even to James, any sort of republican banquet demanded argument; it was not a gathering of crapulent or smug diners. "The obstinate insisting that tweedledum is *not* tweedledee is the bone and marrow of life," he elsewhere asserted. "Look at the Jews and the Scots, with their miserable factions and sectarian disputes, their loyalties and patriotisms and exclusions,—their annals now become a classic heritage, because men of genius took part and sang in them. A thing is important if anyone *think* it important."[21] So James allowed that, were he called to address "the Salvation Army or a miscellaneous popular crowd," he would try to break up and ventilate faiths and help "blow their sickliness and barbarism away."[22] No indifferentist himself, he wanted "the freest competition of the various faiths with one another, and their openest application to

life by their several champions." They "ought to live in pub-
licity, vying with each other."²³

Not only self-described pluralists like James debated "the
one and the many." Father John Courtney Murray, S.J., a recent contender, typified those from other camps who pondered
its implications. Murray was sure that his Catholicism was "the
best and only true" church, yet he respectfully entered what
he called the conversation with others. "Religious pluralism,"
he wrote, "is against the will of God, but it is the human condition; it is written into the script of history. It will not somehow marvelously cease to trouble the City." American
pluralism seemed to him to be especially lamentable. "Many of
the beliefs entertained within society ought not to be believed,
because they are false; nonetheless men believe them." Unlike
the Jamesians, Murray did not believe that the truth would
"always be assured of conquest if only it were subjected to the
unbridled competition of the market place of ideas." Yet the
priest readily agreed with the United States Supreme Court
that it was not the function of government to resolve disputes
between conflicting truths, "all of which claim the final valid-
ity of transcendence." Murray feared not the barbarian who
came to the republican symposium in bearskins with a club in
hand, but the person who wore a Brooks Brothers suit or academic robe and threatened others with scholarly footnotes
that came from his ball-point pen. The priest saw no choice but
to keep the republican debate going, hoping that it might move
some citizens past mutual confusion not to simple agreement
but to better disagreement and from thence to a more civil ar-
gument.²⁴

Just as pluralists and monists shared the table of the Republic, so did those who, like Murray, believed that a *consensus
juris* must help glue society together and those, like James, who
were less sure of this. In his *In Defense of Politics*, Bernard Crick

asked skeptically for representations of this tradition: "Where is the *consensus* in Canada, for instance? Or anywhere, between Catholic, Protestant (High or Low), Muslim, Hindu, Jew, Sceptic, Agnostic, Freethinker, Atheist, and Erastian, who commonly share some common political allegiance—if they take their fundamentals seriously and take them to be directly applicable to politics?" Crick doubted whether any consensus at all could go much further in outline than the merely existential *cri de coeur* of Groucho Marx: "Take care of me. I am the only one I've got."[25]

The majority of Americans, of course, have believed in a consensus, whether somehow achieved or in process, though periodically they call its existence or substance into question. Huge minorities of them, then, set up for themselves the problem of intolerance before they could achieve counterintolerance. What James called their "passional nature" led them to make sectarian choices when options that were living, forced, and momentous faced them. James could sound like an evangelist at altar call: "To say under such circumstance, 'Do not decide, but leave the question open,' is itself a passional decision . . . attended with the risk of losing the truth."[26] So, in a third pairing, citizens also felt called to choose between the conventional sects and those that claimed to represent the very religion of the Republic itself. The latter group today provides the most lively case study for our hypothesis about the nature of counterintolerance at the sort of republican banquet.

FOUR STAGES OF PUBLIC RELIGION

Americans have never begun to agree on what to call the clusters of republican sects. Tocqueville leaned toward "enlightened," and sometimes toward "natural religion" (which the Unitarian former President John Quincy Adams took pains in his presence to distinguish from Unitarianisms), and sometimes to "pure Deism." At Baltimore, Richard Spring Stewart, a physician, fumbled around among words as he told Tocqueville that the vast majority of the enlightened people in America were "truly *believing*" and that they tolerated no anti-Christianity or unbelief. Then he curiously linked "irreligion," or the absence of firm belief, with Deism. Stewart agreed with President Adams that such enlightened Deism had been losing ground for forty years and that by 1831 its progress in the United States was very slow. But historically he could anchor it in the faith of respectable national founders. Jefferson, Franklin, and John Adams were "decidedly deists," though Stewart seemed to think that their colleague George Washington was less decidedly one of their company.[27]

Benjamin Franklin began the advocacy of republican piety when in 1749 he pointed to "the Necessity of a *Publick Religion*." He argued that it would be useful to the public, advantageous in promoting a religious character among private persons, and helpful—was he here twitting the regular sects?—in countering "the mischiefs of superstition."[28] Later, in his *Autobiography*, Franklin defined the substance of public religion when he spelled out "the essentials of every religion." He took pains to exclude all elements of what the Christian majority called saving faith and kept for his canon only "the existence of the Deity, that he made the world, and govern'd it by his Providence; that the most acceptable service of God was the doing good to men; that our souls are immortal; and that all crime will be punished, and virtue rewarded, either here or hereafter." Then, as is well known, he announced his "different degrees of respect" for the sects, depending on the degree to which these essentials were "more or less mix'd with other articles" that did not promote public morale and that did divide citizens.[29]

Just as familiar was the second half of the fundamental

canon that Thomas Jefferson professed in the Declaration of Independence. Fifty years later he was still sure that the "self-evident truths" there stated were "the expression of the American mind."[30] They grounded human equality and the power to govern by consent in a moral order under a divine endowment of inalienable rights and a higher law.[31] Jefferson, who had less use than Franklin for the churches, did allow that "difference of opinion is advantageous to religion. The several sects perform the office of a *censor morum*"[32] and thus contribute to social morale. When, however, Jefferson divorced religion from morals—otherwise, he asked, "whence arises the morality of the Atheist?"[33]—or urged that "it does me no injury for my neighbor to say there are twenty gods, or no God,"[34] he suggested what its proponents often overlook, that republican religion had to be voluntary, no more a part of fundamental law than was churchly religion. Yet even Jefferson worried over how the liberties of a nation would be secure if removed from "their only firm basis, a conviction in the minds of people that these liberties are the gift of God."[35]

Presidents of the United States soon became the priests of public religion. George Washington bade citizens farewell with the view that "religion and morality are indispensable supports"[36]—he significantly differentiated the two and called them twin pillars—for political prosperity. John Adams followed in 1798 with the formal claim that the nation need ask "the protection and the blessing of Almighty God" for the "promotion of that morality and piety without which social happiness cannot exist nor the blessings of a free government be enjoyed."[37] Abraham Lincoln was later to weaken somewhat the Jeffersonian self-evident truths to propositions, yet he still proceeded to call the declaration his creed and to offer his life for it.[38]

The second stage, which concerns us least here because it has less regularly found official support, took diverse shapes in the writings of nineteenth-century literary figures after enlightened Deism faded or lost out to aggressive sectarians. Ralph Waldo Emerson, Henry David Thoreau, Walt Whitman, Herman Melville, and Horace Mann all largely bypassed the historic and divided churches in their proposals. In the interest of social morale they tried to embody a new but often self-contradictory set of public faiths in the form of communal experiments, public schools, or the nation itself. In the end, however, this style of public religion found voice only in the writings of solitary geniuses who attracted reading clienteles, not congregations.

Then, in the middle third of the twentieth century, advocates of a public religion, still united against the churchly sects but disunited about their own alternatives, made new claims. Thus, in 1934, philosopher John Dewey promoted *A Common Faith*, which took democracy as both its setting and its object, over against inherited church religion. Leaving behind the founding fathers, he now wanted a godless religion to turn "explicit and militant." With verbal sleight of hand, he joined the great cloud of witnesses to public religion in the act of conceptually reducing the great number of sects down to only two. "Never before in history," Dewey began his book, "has mankind been so much of two minds, so divided into two camps, as it is today." The educator did not want religious belief any longer to be organized "in a *special* institution within a secular community," evidently not regarding the public school, which would have been the established church of this common faith, to be such an institution. Dewey would allow churches to survive if they dropped their supernaturalism and then celebrated or reinforced naturally in "different ways and with differing symbols" the one "fund of values that are prized and that need to be cherished."[39]

Fear of chaos after World War II led the followers of Dewey to promote social morale through such a naturalist and

democratic faith. J. Paul Williams typically argued that denominational faith was a useless distraction because it was not
"shared with the members of a whole society." After blasting
the churches for being imperial and exclusivist, he called on
government to become so by asking it to teach "the democratic
ideal *as religion*." More alert to ritual than many of his col-
leagues, he hoped democratic society would support such a religion with metaphysical sanctions and ceremonial
reinforcements that would be more effective than those of its
Nazi, Fascist, or Communist counterparts. "Democracy must
become an object of religious dedication. Americans must
come to look on the democratic ideal (not necessarily American
practice of it) as the Will of God or, if they prefer, the Law of
Nature."[40] Horace M. Kallen summarized this case by the
Dewey school: "For the communicants of the democratic faith
it is the religion *of* and *for* religions. . . . [It is] the religion of
religions, all may freely come together in it."[41]

A generation of us who came to maturity in the 1950s
gathered under the banners of Reinhold Niebuhr, John Courtney Murray, and sociologist-theologian Will Herberg to react
against this version of public religion as a "secular humanism"
that was threatening to establish itself. To Herberg, who used
biblical prophetic motifs to judge civic faith most severely of
all, this was a "particularly insidious kind of idolatry." The
"common faith" of American society he thought ought to remain implicit and never be pushed to what he considered a logical conclusion that few others found latent in it. To the mass
of Americans he wrote that civic faith was "not a super-faith
but a common faith," one that made "no pretensions to override or supplant the recognized religions, to which it assigns a
place of great eminence and honor in the American scheme of
things." But, he added ominously, "all the implications are
there. . . ."[42]

In the next decade Will Herberg himself displayed a more

benign view of the now more benign versions of public religion, including the call by Robert N. Bellah in 1967 for Americans to celebrate a civil religion which was "elaborate and well institutionalized," as Bellah thought, "alongside of and rather clearly differentiated from the churches."[43] Bellah, whose program came at the end of an episode that lasted through the third of a century, was friendlier than others to denominational religion. He also emphatically backed off from a religion whose object would be democracy, toward a transcendental theism that evoked texts of Franklin and Lincoln. Then, soon after Bellah had spoken up for this common piety, some renewed religious sects and, more frequently, racial or ethnic groups challenged the very need for consensus and often pressed private interests, neglecting those that promoted social morale. The drastic character of this climatic change in the decade after 1967 occasions a fresh appraisal of the subject.

The "time of troubles"[44] that befell the civic faith is not likely to end calls for public religion. Historians deal with pasts, but it is valid to report on scripts for the future. Many futurists foresee a fourth stage for public religion after the collapse of the present American polity. Typically, economic historian Robert Heilbroner pictured that "in the long run" "business civilization in decline" will not provide for social morale (his term). In the next century, "growing internal and external tension and heightened concern for survival" will call American society "to produce its own values—nationalistic, religious—that will provide a needed new system of beliefs required to replace an outmoded one." Heilbroner expected a "new religious orientation, directed against the canons and precepts of our time, and oriented toward a wholly different conception of the meaning of life and a mode of social organization congenial to the encouragement of that life." A high degree of religious politicism, such as we find in China, will, he thought, "be inescapable." People should at that time deify the state so that it can elevate "the collective and communal destiny of man to the forefront of public consciousness," thus absolutely subordinating private interests to public requirements. Heilbroner, convinced that the passing of the old order would not likely be mourned, looked for little freedom of expression in the forthcoming form of public religion. The republican banquet would certainly end.[45]

Through the years, then, advocates of public religion, while divided over whether it requires a God or not, or whether it should be voluntary or coerced, and though themselves chopped apart by many competing philosophies, have often successfully conveyed the idea that public faith is one big agreed-upon thing over against schismatic church religion. In their eyes the zealous sectarians, who are able to be tolerant only when indifferent, put their energies into religions that are somehow irrelevant to or that distract from or are at least irresponsible about the causes of social morale. Despite the changes, most members of denominations continued to feel at ease at the republican banquet. They regularly moved far beyond the mere respect for "one another's personal sacredness" that circumstances and empathy inspired to some substantive positions that merit analysis.

THREE SUBSTANTIVE POSITIONS

First, the American laity, often without benefit of clergy, as it were, came to differentiate sharply between what we may call ordering faith and saving faith. They did not, of course, all use those terms or invent the hoary distinctions on which they are based. From their sacred books they inherited a wild variety of models, none of them directly applicable to pluralist America. What Beaumont and Tocqueville saw going on at Sing Sing or around Saginaw was an effort of a people who were being forced to rewrite the old charter for Christendom or replace the one that came from the days of Augustine in the fifth century, Thomas Aquinas in the thirteenth, and Calvin and the Puritans in the sixteenth and seventeenth. The Americans, not able or willing to legislate a formally Christian polity, faced a new condition and needed new outlooks.

Though they did not need to cite him, most believed with Augustine that civil society must be rightly ordered *(bene ordinata, bene constituta)*. They took a far more positive view than did he of the sacred dimension of government in the Earthly City. For him, there could arise at best an amoral "republic of a certain kind" in Rome, but even the ruler who was Christian there must despise "those things wherein he is and trust in that wherein he is not yet." On such terms, because *vera justitia*, true justice, belonged only to the City of God, which Rome and America were manifestly not, there could not be a real *res publica*. Only the crabbiest few American prophets have seriously asked, in agreement with Augustine, "Justice removed, what are kingdoms but great robber bands? And what are robber bands but small kingdoms?"[46] Americans might never experience full and true justice, but theirs was a Republic that, as Abraham Lincoln and, one day, their pledge of allegiance to the flag would have it, they saw to be located "under God." In this respect they were closer to the view of Thomas Aquinas, who smuggled into his Augustinian outlook the idea of Aristotle that public values are themselves to be valued, though Americans did not need a Christian state for expression of those values.[47]

Tocqueville came close to developing the new public distinction when he remembered that society itself, having "no future life to hope for or to fear," was not in the business of providing salvation. For that reason, individual citizens banded into groups where "each sect adores the Deity in its own peculiar manner, but all sects preach the same moral law in the name of God."[48] The essentials of all religions served well enough to order government, but they did not save souls, make sad hearts glad, give people wholeness, or provide them with the kind of identity and sense of belonging they craved. For salvation, then, millions of Americans kept on making their choice of the "best and only true sect" for themselves, while, for purposes of order, the canon of Franklin and Jefferson—though not the variation of Dewey and company— agreed with their own, though, they thought, it could never bring salvation at all.

Second, when critics have spotted this form of differentiation, many of them have charged that, because the needs of order for society and salvation for individuals or groups differed, denominational members must always experience contradiction between the public religion in its various manifestations and the particular sects. In a study of anomie, Sebastian de Grazia thus feared a confusion of directives or chaos when people tried to serve two masters.[49] Taking content of belief and the cognitive parts of these faiths for the whole, historian Sidney E. Mead, to further this case, pressed for a resolution of conflict when he reduced Voltaire's many "peaceful and happy religions" to two.[50] Then, fearing, with him, lest "they would destroy each other," Mead hoped that the religion of the Republic alone would prevail, evidently not fearing, as Voltaire had, that the despotism of a single religion "would be terrible."[51]

As recently as 1975 and 1977, Mead wrote of "unresolved tensions" and a "mutual antagonism" between the two "mutually exclusive faiths" of the denominations and the Republic. The two, he thought, had to be "intellectually at war," producing "anxious misery," "wasting sickness," and the "danger of collapse" of the Republic. Along with other evolutionists, Mead believed that when two allied species shared a limited environment "the less successful form" must be forced to migrate or become extinct. Like the French visitors of 1831, he thought and thrice wrote that "religious commitment is an all-or-nothing business" and then pronounced the religion of the particular sects "heretical and schismatic—even un-American!" Mead, finding the counter attitude expressed by "several absolutist Christians toward the 'civil religion,' " cited American folklore in this situation: "This here town just ain't big enough for both of us."

In the eyes of Mead, sectarians still pathetically tried to hold their beliefs in "separate mental compartments" and to live with "split" or "bifurcated" or "schizoid minds." Told that an animal that cannot regurgitate will be killed if it accepts as food what it cannot digest, the historian diagnosed in denominationalists "a psychosomatic indigestion resulting from an inability either to digest the theology on which the practice of religious freedom rests or to regurgitate the practice." The delicate need fear no mess on the tablecloth at the republican banquet; the end of the sectarians, he thought, might come before that. "The prognosis," Mead concluded, "cannot be a happy one."[52]

While possible intellectual contradictions are familiar in religious faiths that allow for paradox, they must be faced. Even William James, despite his zest for "booming, buzzing confusion," thought people could not long tolerate ambiguity. In *Principles of Psychology*, he noted that "we cannot continue to think in two contradictory ways at once."[53] In practical politics, of course, matters are different, as the lively British socialist Jimmy Maxton once observed when he noted that "a man who can't ride two bloody horses at once has no right to a job in the bloody circus."[54] Over the long haul, however, religion called for more than practical adaptation among its professors. The testimony of novelist F. Scott Fitzgerald tantalizes: "The test of a first rate intelligence is the ability to hold two opposed ideas in the mind at the same time, and still retain the ability to function." But those lines occur, we are reminded, in a novel called *The Crack-up*, and a group is not likely to function well or long if posed as Fitzgerald suggests.[55]

Must we, however, even agree that there was such simple contradiction between the functions and content or practice of these two ways of seeing religion as ordering or saving? Most thoughtful sectarians in America showed few signs of recognizing one. They claimed "the essentials of all religion" to be their own for ordering government, but these could not save people. The more modest and less aggressive, and they were legion, also were ready to turn around and say that their particular saving faith could not order the Republic. Reams of documentation show that, after differentiating clearly, most stood with Father Gustave Weigel, S.J., when he observed that "the moral code held by each separate religious community can be reductively unified, but the consistent particular believer wants no reduction."[56] Believers simply translated the generalized deity of a nation "under God" to their own perceived God. Protestant John C. Bennett also urged that "when the word 'God' is used it should mean to the citizens not some common-denominator idea of deity but what they learn about God from their religious traditions."[57] Even the American Council on Education warned them to resist the specter of a saving common core that suggested "a watering down of the several faiths to the point where common essentials appear," since this might "easily lead to a new sect—a public school sect—which would take its place alongside the existing faiths and compete with them."[58]

Denominationalists ordinarily felt little contradiction because they regarded their spiritual antecedents to have been "present at the creation" of public religion. Their religious group, they thought, provided "the essentials of all religions" on which Franklin drew. He himself flattered them by listing among the benefits of a public religion its ability to show "the

Excellency of the CHRISTIAN RELIGION above all others, ancient or modern."[59] Since the canon came from and agreed with the Hebrew Scriptures, Jews did not feel left out, either.[60] But Christians were in the majority. So proud of ownership did they feel that Hannah Arendt finally felt called to remind enthusiastic Christians that they at least ought to send a card of thanks to secularity or modernity for making possible the liberation of revolutionary germs that they claimed but which had been all too hidden during the centuries of Christian dominance.[61]

From Fundamentalists to Unitarians, from the political right to the left, sectarians found their own visions confirmed in men like George Washington or the least-churched president, Abraham Lincoln. Because of Jeffersonian antisectarianism and the clarity of his Deism, however, it took decades before grudging church people could feel at home with that "infidel," though some kinds of Baptists were his allies from the first.[62] While it was true that he left the words of saving Christian faith cut out in snippets on the White House study floor, President Jefferson had pasted together what was left over in a four-language scrapbook called *The Life and Morals of Jesus of Nazareth*.[63] For purposes of order and social morale, how could the Christians repudiate this offspring adopted by someone else—or see a contradiction between it and their churchly ordering faith?

The churches also claimed that they were supporters of republicanism before either the Enlightenment polity or faith emerged. Some of their efforts to produce tickets to the banquet look humorous in retrospect. Thus, before Catholics were secure, Bishop John England and Archbishop John Hughes both pointed to tiny, papally protected, Catholic San Marino as "the most splendid specimen of the purest democracy" for 1,400 years.[64] In 1887 convert Father Isaac Hecker even jostled the Protestants at the banquet-hall door when he claimed that

no republican government ever rose under Protestant ascend-
ancy. "All republics since the Christian era have sprung into
existence under the influence of the Catholic Church"; also,
there existed a necessary bond and relation between the truths
contained in the Declaration of Independence and the revealed
truths of Christianity.[65]

Religious lay people, again often without benefit of
clergy, voiced many ways in which the God of their saving sect
was active in general in ordering the world. Biblically, first of
all: when Jewish Theological Seminary honored Baptist President Harry S. Truman for his part in helping Jews found Israel, he remembered how the Second Isaiah called the Persian
King Cyrus the shepherd or anointed of Yahweh, even though
he was not one of Yahweh's people. Truman showed no ignorance or indifference and certainly no contradiction in his
response of joyful bravado. We are told that he said, ". . . A
man who contributed much? I am Cyrus. I am Cyrus!"[66] The
even more sectarian Jimmy Carter also evidenced no felt contradiction between his saving faith and a cosmic republicanism
when, over oatmeal at the 1978 Presidential Prayer Breakfast,
he told the assembled pious to give thanks for the faiths of Muslim President Anwar el-Sadat and Jewish Prime Minister Men-
achem Begin.

Such improvising laity have come up with a whole catalog
of devices familiar to professional theologians, all designed to
match up the two ways of seeing religion. In an Augustinian
mood, some have found the same God to be active in different
ways through *justitia civilis* or civil righteousness, on one hand,
and through his saving righteousness in the City of God, on
the other. Calvinist and Puritan ideas of their God being active
beyond the sects through "common grace" or his "covenant of
works" have found countless translations.[67] Christians at Boy
Scout banquets, American Civil Liberties Union meetings,
Rotary Club lunches, and Masonic ceremonies often antici-

pated Catholic theologian Karl Rahner with his concept of "the anonymous Christian," without ever yielding their desire to find "onymous" ones in the search for salvation. The idea stated by Paul Tillich that a living religion can break through its particularity at a certain stage[68] took life in the harmless minister-priest-rabbi jokes that pointed to a universalism among people who would never dream of transferring particular care of their souls, or the interpretations of that care, from one of these clerics to another sort. It seems unfair to congratulate professional theologians for finding ways to make things come out right while deriding as indifferent the common people who showed tolerance on principle but remained tenaciously supportive of their particular creeds.

Third, and most ironically, at the republican banquet today the burden of supporting public religion has fallen largely to the very inept and distracted sectarians whom the enlightened expected to see excluding themselves, suffering indigestion, or dying at the banquet door. Through the years the polls showed that the nontheistic versions of John Dewey's common faith had almost no followings.[69] But now we must ask where outside denominational religion are theistic or deistic dimensions of public religion regularly attended to at all. Academic philosophy and political science departments, we must presume, do not teach the canon of public religion as the truth about life. Formal philosophers would dismiss as unverifiably metaphysical the creeds of the enlightened founders and deplore as mystical most later versions of democratic faith. Fortunately, the public philosophy is being revived among thinkers as diverse as Hannah Arendt, John Rawls, Robert Heilbroner, Daniel Bell, Michael Harrington, Robert Nisbet, Robert Nozick, and Irving Kristol, but truly rare is a Peter Berger, who introduces rumors of transcendence, and almost no other of these social philosophers is out to shape social or institutional religious forms.

Public religion is not only intellectual; it must be ritual-
ized. What Elihu Katz and Michael Gurevitch call "the secularization of leisure"[70] has undercut the ritual abode of this
religion in public places. W. Lloyd Warner was still able to see
Memorial Day rites as the American cult of the dead.[71] Since
1959 when he wrote, however, the Congress has turned Memorial Day and most other civil holidays into movable feasts
in order to prolong weekends. In doing so it cut these off from
their historical roots, local communities, or most communal
observances of any sort. Televised football has taken away the
public religious dimensions of Thanksgiving Day, and the pa-
thetic if overblown attempts to restore them at halftime ceremonies are poor substitutes. Public school rites had largely
disappeared before the Supreme Court acted against devotions
in 1962 and 1963. Administrators, when polled, reported that
in exactly 99.44 percent of their districts moral values were
taught, but only 6.4 percent of the Midwest schools and 2.4
percent of the West Coast ones knew anything like homeroom
devotional practices.[72] The people ritually "took God out of the
schools" before the Court did.

The law itself remained the last repository of formal public religion. In 1892 and 1931 Mr. Justice Brewer and Mr. Justice Sutherland continued to call this a religious nation and
Americans a Christian people who acknowledged "with rev-
erence the duty of obedience to the will of God." These were
purely historical notions, as was the first half of the dictum of
Mr. Justice Douglas in 1952 that "we are a religious people."
Douglas had no legal ground for adding that our "institutions
presuppose a Supreme Being," and he slunk away after the immediate dissent by Mr. Justice Black, who protested "invidious
distinctions between those who believe in no religion and those
who do believe."[73]

Thereafter the "wholesomely neutral" Court progres-
sively removed these distinctions while broadening the defi-

nition of what it is to be religious. In 1931 Chief Justice Hughes still defined "the essence of religion" as "belief in a relation to God involving duties superior to those arising from any human relation." By 1965, borrowing a concept from Paul Tillich, the Court backed away from such a slot in theism to declare that "a sincere and meaningful belief which occupies in the life of its possessor a place parallel to that filled by . . . God" among other people would serve civil and legal purposes.[74]

By 1970, in *Welsh* v. *United States*, the Court went still further, judging that a conscientious objector to military service did not even have to claim to be godlessly religious, so long as the Court judged that his or her "moral, ethical, or religious belief about what is right and wrong" was "held with the strength of traditional religious convictions." The last trace of religious substance was now gone. Mr. Justice Harlan complained that in 1965 the Court had engaged in surgery but in 1970 "performed a lobotomy." He then went on anyhow to write that Congress "cannot draw the line between theistic or nontheistic beliefs on the one hand and the secular beliefs on the other" in issues.[75] At last the issue was bare and bald for all to see: from the beginning in the United States public religion was itself a congeries of voluntary sects, some of them privileged, but none of them ever established by law.

THE REPUBLICAN BANQUET TODAY

In 1950 the United States Supreme Court invaded the American sanctum with its dictum that the law knows no heresy and is committed to the support of no dogma. This judgment made visible an aspect of American common life that metaphorically parallels what Pompey was said to have found in 63 B.C. when he finally crashed into the Temple Holy of Holies in Jerusalem: it was empty.[76] The American sectarians of republican and denominational religion alike have, of course, persistently sneaked their own sacral appointments and scrolls into the shrine for their particular rituals and reflection. Enough of them have agreed on essentials of republican order that they can plausibly speak of consensus. Some have done so with such enthusiasm that the critics within their camps faulted churches themselves for promoting civil idolatry. Robert Bellah wryly remarked that "perhaps the real animus of the religious critics has been not so much against the civil religion in itself but against its pervasive and dominating influence within the sphere of church religion."[77] During the national bicentennial, denominations arranged religious civil ceremonies while their own prophets criticized them. The surrounding society more regularly neglected such rites and instead invited the public to watch the tall ships in the Hudson or the fireworks above the Potomac.

Why had the churches taken over so many seats at the republican banquet? It takes no originality to point out that selfish interests motivated the beginnings of their involvement. In the Massachusetts Election Sermon of 1780, the Reverend Samuel Cooper was already calling for a "happy union of all denominations" in support of national government because it provided equal protection to all. "Warm parties upon civil or religious matters,"[78] however, were injurious to the state. In 1958, Father Gustave Weigel, S.J., feared what some have called "repressive tolerance" because he saw the secular society "trying to make a deal with the churches," saying "give us your unswerving support in the pursuit of the objectives we have before us; in return we will cover you with honor."[79] Then, in 1961, William Lee Miller went on to point out that because tax-exempt religious groups could not advertise their worth as peddlers of dogma or mysticism they had to tout their value as agents of social morale—whether they were revivalist or modernist or representative of the sects of "the deistic and rationalist strand."[80] And so, indeed, they have presented themselves.

After this self-interested beginning, the partakers at the banquet did not simply proceed to write out invitation lists for competitors. Most of them at first found each other to be at best what James once called "half-delightful company."[81] In 1954 Perry Miller was crass enough to remind readers that "we got a variety of sects as we got a college catalog: the denominations and the sciences multiplied until there was nothing anybody could do about them." So citizens gave out tickets to the common table, called the result freedom, and found "to our vast delight, that by thus negatively surrendering we could congratulate ourselves on a positive and heroic victory. So we stuck the feather in our cap and called it Yankee Doodle."[82] High principle, if it came, had to arrive later, after respect for persons had developed.

Through the years the guest list of participants kept growing. Even today, however, when groups overtly fuse their saving faith with ordering faith, they exclude themselves or are rebuffed by others. Jehovah's Witnesses are the classic case; they see human governments to be ordered by Satan, and they salute no flags of earthly states.[83] The Nation of Islam or "Black Muslim" movement began as an outsider with similar views of the white majority but now is knocking on the door.[84] In order to resist being swallowed up or abused, some religious American Indians are turning down tardy and grudging invitations by other religions to partake.[85] Not only in Kanawha County, West Virginia, have fundamentalists sniffed unwelcome natural religion in textbooks on evolution or atheistic communism in public schoolrooms. They then either stage their own banquets or, like silent film star Gloria Swanson, they come to the public one but insist on bringing all their own food.

Other groups begin by first ignoring the gathering, but

they join it later on terms they learned from the Enlightenment. The Baptists and Quakers are among these. Originally they were what George Santayana called "pensive or rabid apostles of liberty" who sought "liberty for themselves to be just so, and to remain just so for ever," vehemently defying anybody who might for the sake of harmony ask them to be a little different. In the course of time they learned that for liberty they needed what Santayana called "a certain vagueness of soul, together with a great gregariousness and tendency to be moulded by example and by prevalent opinion." Santayana also knew what many have always overlooked: that it took passion to defend the very idea of the banquet. Enthusiasts for democratic liberty, he said, were "not everybody's friends" because they were enemies of "what is deepest and most primitive in everybody" and since they inspired "undying hatred in every untamable people and every absolute soul."[86]

The career of the Mormons best illustrates the process of change. British visitor D.W. Brogan rightly found them to be the only genuine example of religious persecution in modern America because they followed two sacred books.[87] Their Book of Mormon both looked and was different from the Bible in its ordering of society. Though founders Joseph Smith and Brigham Young were super-American people who regarded the founding documents of the nation as being inspired from on high, they insisted these were only temporary charters until God's Kingdom, in Mormon hands, would achieve "domination over all the earth to the ends thereof."[88] When the Latter-Day Saints later dropped the offending practice of polygamy and muted their claims of the kingdom, they finally were welcome to the banquet as patriots—by fellow-citizens who still remain as hostile as ever if they see Mormons in the act of being aggressive about their way of salvation.

Most debate at the banquet occurs when someone spots another sect apparently mingling elements of its particular saving outlook with the general essentials of ordering faith power. Here the Catholic case is most instructive. The example of San Marino did not make Catholics secure in the eyes of others. Many scores of years of participation beyond suspicion in republican life in America did not help. Not until 1960, when one of their own became president, were they themselves seen to be thoroughly at home. After 1965, when the Second Vatican Council, acting on American impetus, acknowledged a development of Catholic doctrine and declared religious freedom to be a right, there was no longer any basis for complaints of antirepublicanism against official Catholicism.[89] Even so, as in the case when Catholics or anyone else today become accused of trying to legislate what looks to others like a particularistic element of their faith—such as prohibitions against the abortion of fetuses—there develops the kind of confusion Murray feared, sometimes the clarified disagreement he hoped for, and on rarest occasions a higher level of civil argument.

The republican banquet, be it remembered, is not the only show in town. Many citizens still choose the enlightened sects of public religion, and many millions of them select one sect or another of denominational religion, thereafter often to put few energies into the common weal. But millions more who share some beliefs are not available as part of any kind of social force, because they have made religion a wholly private, individual, and even invisible affair and thus no contributor to the causes of social morale. Around them are self-described secular people who ignore the whole debate on all its terms. The courts have been clear: one need not believe in a *consensus juris*, and certainly not in a religious base for one, in order to be a full citizen, in the legally responsible senses. Those who are partakers at the republican banquet have shown myriad ways in which they wish to be responsible both to their focused visions and to the common good, without being superficial or indifferent about their life and thought. It is not now possible, nor will it ever be, to chart the infinite number of ways they have done so. Like Beaumont after Sing Sing, thoughtful people shall find puzzles remaining. We, too, stand humbly at the side of the French visitor to declare that we "would gladly know" more about the marvelous and troubling ways of a contentious republican people.

Notes

1. Quoted by George Wilson Pierson, *Tocqueville in America* (Garden City: Doubleday, 1959), p. 70 (abridged by Dudley C. Lunt from *Tocqueville and Beaumont in America* [1938]).

2. Alexis de Tocqueville, *Journey to America* (Garden City: Doubleday, 1971), p. 290.

3. Quoted by Pierson, p. 99.

4. Quoted *ibid.*, p. 139; cf. Tocqueville, p. 15.

5. Quoted by Anson Phelps Stokes and Leo Pfeffer, *Church and State in the United States* (New York: Harper and Row, 1964), p. 61.

6. Quoted by Pierson, p. 139.

7. Quoted by Walter J. Ong, S.J., *American Catholic Crossroads* (New York: Macmillan, 1959), p. 20.

8. Quoted by Tocqueville, p. 12.

9. Quoted by Pierson, p. 132.

10. Quoted *ibid.*, p. 70. Robert Heilbroner (*Business Civilization in Decline* [New York: W. W. Norton & Co., 1976], pp. 112ff.) develops the concept of "social morale."

11. Quoted by Pierson, p. 100.

12. Tocqueville, pp. 395ff.

13. *Ibid.*, p. 270; cf. Pierson, p. 203.

14. John Dewey, *Human Nature and Conduct* (New York: Modern Library, 1930), p. 226.

15. Nathaniel Ward, *The Simple Cobler of Aggawam in America*, ed. P.M. Zall (Lincoln: University of Nebraska Press, 1969), p. 10; the first edition appeared in 1647.

16. For a sampling of the belief of peasants and bourgeois in France just before this period, see Bernard Groethuysen, *The Bourgeois: Catholicism vs. Capitalism in Eighteenth Century France* (New York: Holt, Rinehart & Winston, 1968).

17. Perry Miller, "From the Covenant to the Revival," in James Ward Smith and A. Leland Jamison, eds., *The Shaping of American Religion* (Princeton: Princeton University Press, 1961), I: 365.

18. William James, *The Will to Believe* (New York: Dover, 1956), p. 270. The image of a republic appeared frequently in the writings of William James. H.S. Levinson of Stanford University traced it in *Science, Metaphysics, and the Chance of Salvation* (Missoula, Mont.: Scholar's Press, 1978), p. 116. Even James' vision of a savable world is "conceived after a social analogy," that of a federal republic, which is "constituted as a 'pluralism of independent powers.' " James, according to Levinson, works out three analogies between the world and a federal republic: variety, novelty, and activity in universes of discourse and practice. Federal republics are constituted to generate social accommodation, the assimilation of novel proposals, and purposes held in common by constituents of this universe.

19. Cited by Sidney E. Mead, *The Nation with the Soul of a Church* (New York: Harper and Row, 1975), p. 39.

20. Gabriel Marcel, *Creative Fidelity* (New York: Farrar, Straus & Co., 1964), pp. 211, 214.

21. Quoted by Ralph Barton Perry, *The Thought and Character of William James* (Boston: Little, Brown & Co., 1935), II:266ff.

22. James, p. x.

23. *Ibid.*, p. xii.

24. John Courtney Murray, S.J., *We Hold These Truths: Catholic Reflections on the American Proposition* (New York: Sheed and Ward, 1960), pp. 23, 74, 129, 12, 15.

25. Bernard Crick, *In Defense of Politics* (Baltimore: Penguin Books, 1964), p. 176.

26. James, pp. 11, 3, 11.

27. Tocqueville (n. 2 above), pp. 70ff.

28. Chester E. Jorgenson and Frank Luther Mott, eds., *Benja-*

min Franklin: Representative Selections, with Introduction, Bibliography, and Notes (New York: Hill and Wang, 1962), p. 203.

29. *Ibid.*, pp. 69ff.

30. Thomas Jefferson, *The Writings of Thomas Jefferson*, ed. Paul Leicester Ford (New York: G.P. Putnam's Sons, 1899), X: 343.

31. See the discussion on this point in Joseph F. Costanzo, S.J., *This Nation Under God* (New York: Herder and Herder, 1964), pp. 29ff.

32. Thomas Jefferson, *Notes on the State of Virginia* (New York: Harper and Row, 1964), p. 153.

33. Adrienne Koch and William Peden, *The Life and Selected Writings of Thomas Jefferson* (New York: Random House, 1944) p. 637.

34. Jefferson, *Notes on the State of Virginia*, p. 152.

35. *Ibid.*, p. 156.

36. John C. Fitzpatrick, ed., *The Writings of George Washington* (Washington, D.C.: Superintendent of Documents, 1931–44), XXXV: 258.

37. James D. Richardson, ed., *A Compilation of the Messages and Papers of the Presidents, 1789–1897* (Washington, D.C.: Government Printing Office, 1897), I: 258.

38. For an important discussion of Lincoln's use of the declaration, see Glen E. Thurow, *Abraham Lincoln and American Political Religion* (Albany: State University of New York Press, 1976), chap. 4 and esp. pp. 72ff.

39. John Dewey, *A Common Faith* (New Haven: Yale University Press, 1934), pp. 87, 1, 61, 82.

40. J. Paul Williams, *What Americans Believe and How They Worship*, rev. ed. (New York: Harper & Row, 1962), pp. 486, 488, 491ff., 484.

41. Horace M. Kallen, "Democracy's True Religion," *Saturday Review of Literature* (July 28, 1951).

42. Will Herberg, *Protestant, Catholic, Jew* (Garden City: Doubleday, 1955), p. 102.

43. Donald R. Cutler, ed., *The Religious Situation, 1968* (Boston: Beacon Press, 1968) is one of a number of places in which Bellah published his essay "Civil Religion in America"; see p. 331.

44. *Ibid.*, p. 351.

45. Heilbroner, *Business Civilization in Decline*, pp. 112, 117, 119, 120.

46. Herbert A. Deane, *The Political and Social Ideas of St. Augustine* (New York: Columbia University Press, 1963), pp. 125, 122, 119ff., 127; see chap. 4 and esp. p. 120. I have found Deane's interpretation more convincing than that of Charles H. McIlwain.

47. See the discussion of this point in Glen Caudill Dealy, *The Public Man* (Amherst: University of Massachusetts Press, 1977), pp. 76ff. and esp. 77n.

48. Alexis de Tocqueville, *Democracy in America* (New York: Alfred A. Knopf, 1954), I: 314.

49. Sebastian de Grazia, *The Political Community: A Study of Anomie* (Chicago: University of Chicago Press, 1948), pp. 45ff.

50. Mead, *The Nation with the Soul of a Church*, pp. ix, 19.

51. Voltaire is quoted by Stokes and Pfeffer, *Church and State*, p. 23.

52. Mead, pp. ix, 5, 33, 37, 115, 22, 124, 125, 27; interspersed also are sequences of quotations from Mead, *The Old Religion in the Brave New World* (Berkeley: University of California Press, 1977), pp. 2, 3, 42, 1.

53. William James, *The Principles of Psychology* (New York: Henry Holt & Co., 1904), II: 290.

54. Quoted by Crick, *In Defense of Politics*, p. 138.

55. Quoted by Charles Hampden-Turner, *Radical Man* (Cambridge, Mass.: Schenkman Publishing Co., 1970), p. 39. Sidney Mead, with manifest delight, called my attention to the "crack-up" context.

56. Gustave Weigel, S.J., "The Church and the Public Conscience," *Atlantic Monthly* 210 (August, 1962), 116–17; quoted by Philip Kurland in *Church and State: The Supreme Court and the First Amendment* (Chicago: University of Chicago Press, 1975), p. 31.

57. John C. Bennett, *Christians and the State* (New York: Scribner's, 1958), p. 9.

58. Quoted by Kurland, p. 31.

59. Jorgenson and Mott, *Benjamin Franklin*, p. 203.

60. Typical of Jewish works on this subject is Abraham I. Katsh, *The Biblical Heritage of American Democracy* (New York: Ktav, 1977).

61. Hannah Arendt, *On Revolution* (New York: Viking Press, 1963), pp. 18–20.

62. For an example, see L.F. Greene, ed., *The Writings of John Leland* (1945; reprint ed., New York: Arno Press and New York Times Book Company, 1969).

63. See the discussion in Daniel J. Boorstin, *The Lost World of Thomas Jefferson* (Boston: Beacon Press, 1948), pp. 159ff.

64. Cited by Dorothy Dohen, *Nationalism and American Catholicism* (New York: Sheed and Ward, 1967), pp. 94, 96.

65. Isaac Hecker, *The Church and the Age* (New York: Catholic World, 1887), pp. 84, 71, 79, 96ff.; see Dohen, p. 102.

66. Quoted by Franklin H. Littell, *The Crucifixion of the Jews* (New York: Harper and Row, 1975); this does not appear in his prepared remarks, and I have not been able to confirm it.

67. On "common grace," see John T. McNeill, ed., *Calvin: Institutes of the Christian Religion* (Philadelphia: Westminster Press, 1960), I: 273. For an example of how a kind of "law of nature" enters the Puritan tradition, see the discussion of John Preston in Perry Miller, *Errand into the Wilderness* (Cambridge, Mass.: Harvard University Press, 1956), pp. 74ff.

68. Paul Tillich, *Christianity and the Encounter of World Religions* (New York: Columbia University Press, 1963), p. 97; on the concept of "anonymous Christian" in Karl Rahner, see the full discussion, Robert J. Schreiter, "The Anonymous Christian and Christology," in *Occasional Bulletin of Missionary Research* 2, no. 1 (January 1978), 2ff.

69. I have reference here to the way Gallup polls and others show well over ninety percent of the people expressing themselves in theistic or deistic terms.

70. For a study of comparable issues in Israel, see Elihu Katz and Michael Gurevitch, *The Secularization of Literature: Culture and Communication in Israel* (Cambridge, Mass.: Harvard University Press, 1976).

71. W. Lloyd Warner, *The Family of God* (New Haven: Yale University Press, 1961), pp. 155–260 (based on writings from 1959).

72. Richard B. Dierenfeld, *Religion in American Public Schools* (Washington, D.C.: Public Affairs Press, 1962), pp. 45, 56, passim.

73. A discussion of the role of law in public religion and references to these court cases appear in Phillip E. Hammond, "Religious Pluralism and Durkheim's Integration Thesis," in Allan W. Eister, ed., *Changing Perspectives in the Scientific Study of Religion* (New York: John Wiley & Sons, 1974), pp. 129ff.

74. Richard E. Morgan, *The Supreme Court and Religion* (New York: Free Press, 1972), p. 198; see also Kurland, *Church and State*, p. 74.

75. Hammond, p. 131; Morgan, p. 170; and Kurland, p. 179, include references to the cited cases.

76. Daniel J. Boorstin (*The Genius of American Politics* [Chicago: University of Chicago Press, 1953], p. 170) first compared the situation.

77. Bellah, "American Civil Religion," in Cutler, *The Religious Situation, 1968*, p. 347.

78. Quoted by Franklin P. Cole, ed., *They Preached Liberty* (Indianapolis: Liberty Fund, Inc., 1976), p. 163.

79. Gustave Weigel, S.J., "The Present Embarrassment of the Church," in John Cogley, ed., *Religion in America* (Cleveland: Meridian Books, 1958), p. 234.

80. William Lee Miller, "American Religion and American Political Attitudes," in Smith and Jamison, *The Shaping of American Religion*, II: 93–95.

81. Perry, *The Thought and Character of William James*, II: 268.

82. Cited by Robert T. Handy, "The American Tradition of Religious Freedom: An Historical Analysis," *Journal of Public Law* 13 (1964), 247–66, quotation from p. 251.

83. On Jehovah's Witnesses, see Morgan, pp. 58–74.

84. On the early years of the Black Muslims, see C. Eric Lincoln, *The Black Muslims in America* (Boston: Beacon Press, 1961).

85. A typical expression is Vine Deloria, Jr., *God Is Red* (New York: Grosset & Dunlap, 1973).

86. George Santayana, *Character and Opinion in the United States* (Garden City: Doubleday, 1956), pp. 135ff.

87. See Cutler, *The Religious Situation, 1968*, p. 357.

88. Quoted by Klaus Hansen, *Quest for Empire* (East Lansing: Michigan State University Press, 1967), p. 43.

89. John Courtney Murray develops the theme of "development" in his writings on this subject; see Walter M. Abbott, S.J., *The Documents of Vatican II* (New York: Herder and Herder/Association Press, 1966), pp. 672ff.

Notes on the Contributors

RICHARD J. BERNSTEIN is professor of philosophy at Haverford College. He is the author of *The Restructuring of Social and Political Theory*, *Praxis and Action*, and *Beyond Objectivism and Relativism*.

FRANKLIN I. GAMWELL is dean of the Divinity School of the University of Chicago and associate professor of ethics and ministerial studies. He is the author of *Beyond Preference*.

ROBIN W. LOVIN is associate professor of ethics and society at the Divinity School of the University of Chicago and director of the Project on Religion and American Public Life. He is the author of *Christian Faith and Public Choices*.

MARTIN E. MARTY is Fairfax M. Cone Distinguished Service Professor at the Divinity School of the University of Chicago. His many books on religion and American life include *The Public Church* and *Pilgrims in Their Own Land*.

DOUGLAS STURM is professor of religion and political science at Bucknell University. He is a past president of the Society of Christian Ethics.

DAVID TRACY is professor of theology at the Divinity School of the University of Chicago. He is the author of *Blessed Rage for Order* and *The Analogical Imagination*.

DATE DUE

MAY 10 '89			